THINK
WHERE YOU'RE
GOING

THE MUST-HAVE BOOK FOR NEW GRADUATES SEEKING SUCCESS IN LIFE

By Mike Eltgroth

BeachPath
Press, LLC

ISBN 978-0-9961745-0-3
(paperback)

First Edition, 2015

BeachPath Press, LLC
Visit us online at beachpathpress.com

Dedications

To the family and friends that have helped me
to succeed and especially to the young people in my life
that have inspired this work, I say thank you.

To my wife, who has given unwavering support as I
seek my own success in life, I could not have done this
without you.

CONTENTS

Preface

Now What?

One night many years ago I found myself lying on the carpet and staring at the ceiling. I felt incredibly anxious. My hands clutched the carpet, either to keep my stomach from flipping over or to keep the room from spinning. I wasn't sure which one. My mind was a blur of thoughts that ping-ponged from confident and positive to completely disastrous. My father thought I was crazy, but my friends seemed to think that what I was doing was a good idea. If things went wrong, however, things could turn out badly. I could get sued, lose lots of money, or both. What had I done to put myself in such a mind-boggling predicament? I had just put an offer on a house for the first time, and I was terrified.

This wasn't just any house though. This was an up-and-down duplex. I intended to live in the top half and rent out the bottom unit. I was young, only a few years out of college, and had just moved to this new town about a year earlier. For that first year I had rented a townhouse first and then a free-standing single-family home. The home had been a parish house, a little house right next to a church. The house was nice, but its location resulted in a long commute and the higher rent payment began to take a toll on me. A friend of mine owned several small rental buildings in town. As I learned more about what he had done, it seemed to make a lot of sense to me. At about the same time I had also begun reading a series of books on gaining wealth through real estate investing that was written by a popular author. It was the guy with two dads, Robert Kiyosaki. My juvenile brain had at least a spark of realization that working at a traditional job until the day I died didn't seem like a great plan for me. No, there had to be another way. As I asked questions and read books, all of what they said seemed to add up in my young mind. I certainly didn't need a free-standing house, since I had no wife or kids. I didn't own much stuff, but renting felt like I was being robbed in some way. I had a friend who had made the duplex idea work, and as luck would have it, I had a pretty good real estate agent. So why was I lying on the floor in a terrified daze? Fear of the unknown.

The unknown was in all the details involved in buying a house and my lack of understanding them. My parents are wonderful people whom I love dearly, and they did their best to raise me well. By most accounts, they did a pretty good job since I am self-sufficient and not a complete jerk. They tried to teach me what they knew about the world to prepare me for it in the best way they knew how. My parents, unfortunately, aren't financial wizards and had never dabbled much in real estate. I don't think they ever actually purchased a house of their own until I was at least 10 years old and never had any rental income property because we were a military family and moved often. When I told my father that I wanted to buy a duplex, he was not exactly encouraging. He shared some of the same fears I did about it possibly turning into a disaster. Could I make the payments? What if the renters were a problem? What if they didn't pay? What if I lost my job at this startup company I worked for? What if the house lost value and I had to sell it? What if, what if? Thanks, Dad, but you're not helping.

In the end, I did buy that duplex and owned it and another larger property for about seven years before I finally sold them and made a nice profit. In the more than 15 years since that agonizing night on the carpet, I have learned a lot more about life through work, family, friends, books, investment experiences, and other means. I made mistakes and I made some good choices. One question that often popped into my mind when I learned another life lesson along the way was, "Why didn't somebody tell me this stuff earlier?" Why wasn't there a class or some kind of user's manual on life handed out at high school or college graduation? Would I have even read such a thing if someone had given it to me back then? It's hard to say. I hope that I would have. Eventually, though, I probably would have turned to it, dusted it off, and kicked myself for not reading it earlier.

I hope this book will be that book for you—the book that I never got. This isn't the be-all, end-all guide to life and is naturally full of a lot of my own experiences and opinions, but it's something. It's something to get you started. It will show you how our society works and what is probably waiting for you depending on how you choose to think, how you act, and what you value.

A few years ago my cell phone began to fail so I went to my local store in search of a replacement. As I pondered the displays of the latest technology promising to solve all of the problems that I didn't even know I had, I happened to notice a car pull into a parking space right outside the window that I was near. The car had seen better days, and from the looks of it probably only had a year or two of life left in it. A young couple, likely in their late teens or very early twenties, exited the car and came in to the store. It was obvious to me that they probably didn't have a lot of money, but they proceeded to examine the latest and most expensive phones in the store. Over the next half hour I watched as the young man purchased one of these phones along with a high end data plan. I didn't hear the exact figures, but I could only assume that the phone and data plan were going to cost him close to $1,500 in the first year alone. I winced.

Observing this transaction got me to thinking about the differences between that young man and myself. There I was, a 35 year old professional, looking for the cheapest phone that I could get while he was doing the exact opposite. Did he understand the possible impacts of that choice on the rest of his life? Did he even consider it? What did he value most in his life compared to what I did? Would he ever come to regret that purchase or was he doing exactly what he wanted to do? What was he thinking?

Much of our life's journey is driven by our own choices. The more you know about the probable outcomes of your choices, the more prepared you will be. Where do you want your life to go? Do you want a nice house in the suburbs with 2.3 kids and a new car? Do you want to stop working at 28 years old with enough money to never work again? Do you want to bounce from minimum-wage job to minimum-wage job living paycheck to paycheck, but have really fun friends, a cool phone and few responsibilities? It is pretty much up to you.

This book is not a how-to book. This book is about letting you know a little about how the world you are about to enter actually works and what your decisions, thoughts, and actions might lead to. This is more of a book on expectations. You shouldn't expect to realize your dreams unless you think and act in ways that will lead you toward them. You are free to pick your path, and probably more importantly, you are free to change your path if things haven't lived up to your expectations. To do that, you'll have to *think* about your life. If you start there, you'll probably get to where you want to go.

-Mike Eltgroth

Introduction

A man who dares to waste one hour of time
has not discovered the value of life.
-Charles Darwin

Congratulations on your graduation! I'm certain that this is the culmination of a long, hard-fought battle in which you have come out victorious. Well done! But of course this battle is just one of many and is by no means the end of the war. There still remains the vast majority of your life ahead of you, with many exhilarating highs, troublesome lows, and the daily, weekly, and yearly flow of your journey. For many of you, the last several years have been a time of tremendous growth. You've learned about people, relationships, time, consequences, money and loans, how to party, how to piss people off and then clear the air, how long cold pizza will last, and maybe, just maybe, a little about history and algebra.

When you finally walk out of the building on your last day or walk down the steps of the stage with that diploma in your hand, what is next for you? You might have it all planned out with a job lined up and moving boxes stuffed and taped. Maybe not. Maybe you have no plans at all and are full of trepidation. Perhaps you are just full of excitement at your new-found freedom and the endless possibilities that stretch out before you like an ocean. Before you dive in and start swimming, though, wouldn't it be helpful to know what is lurking out there? Dolphins, sure, but sharks as well. Playful otters and painful jellyfish. Gentle rolling waves and dangerous currents. Life is an amazing thing, and knowing what to expect can make a huge difference in achieving your success in it.

No doubt you have been greatly influenced in how you think about life by the things and people who surround you. Many of these influences are well meant, useful, and accurate. Many are not. There are dozens of books out there about investing, interviewing, entrepreneurship, influencing people, and becoming successful in the field of your choice. There are some great inspirational titles as well. I have read a selection of these books myself over the years, but I always felt a little cheated when I did. I constantly had nagging thoughts like these: "Why am I finding out about this now?" Sometimes I'd think, "Oh, well that makes sense to me now, but why didn't anybody tell me this stuff up front?" I'd even ask myself, "Why did I learn so much about organic chemistry in school and virtually nothing about the day-to-day workings of life and our society?" I'd think, "If I had only known better, I would have done X, Y, or Z instead of A, B, and C."

So that is what this book is for. I want to give you a little insight into the workings of the world. It's a bit of a leg up or a head start that most people get from a special school: the school of hard knocks. You'll likely learn many of the same lessons that I have learned as you go through life, but this book could shave years or decades off of your learning curve.

I'm giving you the book that I wish I had been given many years ago to help me clarify my thoughts and plans. To be clear, this is not a get-rich-quick book or even a how-to-get-rich book. Rather, this is a book about figuring out where you want to go and determining the best way to get started. It's about your choices and where they might lead. I'm not going to tell you what to do with your life. It's your life, and you can do whatever you want to with it. I just want to give you some information so that you can make conscious choices about the path of your life. You shouldn't have regrets or blame somebody else if one day you look around and find that you don't like what you see. I want you to start making your choices with a bigger picture in mind than you likely have right now.

The path of your life is largely up to one person, you, and the effects of your choices on your future are already taking shape. Looking back and wishing that somebody would have told you something 10 years earlier is a bitter and all-too-common pill to swallow in life.

It's quite likely that someone gave you this book as a gift. In that case, consider yourself very fortunate. The person who gave you this book cares enough about you to give you some advice today that might last a lifetime. If you acquired this book on your own, consider yourself even more fortunate. I say that because obtaining this book by your own choice means that you are already thinking about some very important things. Paying attention to such things puts you among a minority of people, and that's a very good thing that will become clear later in the book. So whether the book was a gift or a choice on your part, I hope your reading it is the beginning of a fantastic journey for you. Graduation is here, and your life is stretching out before you. The sun is just up over the horizon, and you are finally on your way. Let's get going!

I've split this book into three main parts. Part 1 is about things. Things most often come from money. Money is a big part of our society, and like it or not, you're going to be dealing with it for the rest of your life. In this part of the book, I give you a little information, just a little, about money and then talk about how it is used. If you aren't that interested in money or numbers right now, please stick with me for just a few chapters. They are short, but important, and they might have a large impact on your future.

Part 2 is about the other part of life, people. This includes you and the people with whom you interact, either by choice or by circumstance. Common threads and themes run through our dealings with ourselves and others. These threads and themes include (1) what is valued, (2) one's thoughts about time and money, and (3) one's attitude. In part 2 you'll learn about these threads and themes so that you can keep them in mind as you navigate through the next phases of your life.

Part 3 includes the last three chapters which cover getting started on your journey, managing changes along the way and a final wrap up. In addition to the main parts, there are HIGHLIGHTS scattered throughout the book. These HIGHLIGHTS are important snippets of information that help reinforce what you have read and act as a quick reference or reminder as you thumb through the book later.

THINK WHERE YOU'RE GOING

Part 1

Stuff

THINK WHERE YOU'RE GOING

1

Success

Success is getting what you want.
Happiness is wanting what you get.
-Anonymous

What is Success?

Close your eyes and picture success. What does it look like to you? Money, cars, big houses, travel, freedom? Perhaps you picture mastering a musical instrument, starting a foundation, or saving lives. Success is a term that is thrown about frequently and many, if not most, people equate success with money, power, or prestige. Online dictionaries commonly define success as the attainment of wealth, respect, or fame. Is that really what it is? The simple answer is yes and no. The answer to the question, "What is success?" depends on whom you ask. Ask any two people for an answer, and while they might have similar views of what success is, their answers won't be exactly the same.

Another definition of success is the broader, and more appropriate, version which is the attainment of the attempt. Stated another way, if you got what you were after then you were successful. If Tim wanted to win the football game and he did, then he was successful. If Tina wanted to skip class and slept right through it, then she was successful. If Tim buys that sports car that he has been lusting after, then he has succeeded. Success depends entirely on you and what you are trying to do.

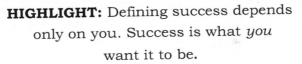

HIGHLIGHT: Defining success depends only on you. Success is what *you* want it to be.

Pressure

As we stated before, a common definition of success is having fancy things, money, or power. This definition is not entirely correct, but the underlying principle often is. We'll get to that part a bit later on. Let's face it, we live in an increasingly materialistic and interconnected world. The past hundred years have been an amazing time of technological growth. Our systems and machines allow us to produce goods more efficiently and faster than ever before. Information is readily available, financial and commercial transactions are instantaneous, and fortunes can be made or lost at the drop of a hat. This age of rapid and widespread communication coupled with an abundance of desirable products can create a lot of pressure to over-consume or do things that really aren't true to who we are.

People often desire the nice things that we have created and figured out how to produce at reasonable costs. Nice things are those things that help us either physically or emotionally and are of good quality. If you're going to buy something, you might as well get the best, right? When we acquire things, we frequently get the best that is available to us for one of three reasons. We want the best performance, the best value, or the best status that we can get. We often get the best that we convince ourselves we can afford, whether we really can or not.

My father used to tell me that if I was going to buy a tool I should get the best that I could. I have found that to be pretty good advice most of the time. If I have a need for something to solve a problem, then why not get the best solution so the problem gets fixed well and doesn't return? If it does happen to return, then I still have a good tool to fix it with. That works pretty well for getting things that I need. Yet there aren't many things that I actually need. There are lots of things that I want, sure, but not many that I truly need. The things that we want in life can satisfy a desire to feel a certain emotion, such as excitement, success, acceptance, or enjoyment.

Buying things that you feel pressured to in order to make you look successful or be accepted by others can lead you to buy things that you really don't need or can't even afford. And worst of all, you might be buying things to impress other people who don't matter that much to your life anyway. Success should be something that you define through your own view of the world and what is important to you. We are surrounded by everyone else's image of success, so it is easy to assume that those images must be correct. It seems only natural to believe that success means having lots of expensive things if that is the image that you see a

24

hundred times a day on TV, in movies, on the Internet, or in your neighbor's driveway.

We are social creatures, and acceptance is important to us. The pressure to conform can be very strong. What should also be important to you are your own desires and your own vision of success. If your vision of success also matches what you feel pressured to do, then go for it. If not, you will need to examine your values closely to create the life that you want instead of the life that you think society says that you should have. Don't assume that you have to follow the path that everyone else appears to be taking. The pressure to conform and follow the group can be intense, but you must decide if that is really right for you. There's more on your values and the appearance of success coming in Part 2.

HIGHLIGHT: The images of success that you see daily might not be what you really need or even desire.

What Do You Want Out of Life?

Let's talk about you and your preferences for a few minutes. What do you want out of life? What would it take for you to feel successful? What do you value? What are your goals? Take the short quiz in this section and write your answers next to the question or on a piece of paper that you will keep with the book. I know, I know. School's done so why do you have to take another quiz?! Trust me, this is where it starts to get really important. There are no right or wrong answers here, so just answer honestly. After you take the quiz, determine your scores. We'll work with your answers in chapter 6.

1. If you were given $5,000 right now, what would you do with the money?
    a. Buy a new stereo for your car.
    b. Pay off a credit card and buy some new clothes.
    c. Save it.

2. Which would you pick?
    a. A pay cut of 50%, but work 75% less.
    b. A pay raise of 15% that requires 25% overtime.
    c. A pay raise of 50% that requires 50% overtime.

3. The last time you thought about what you wanted to be when you grew up was:
    a. In third grade.
    b. Last year.
    c. Yesterday.

4. Your dream house is:
   a. Anything that is paid for.
   b. Full of kids.
   c. A big mansion.

5. Do you smoke?
   a. Yes.
   b. No.
   c. Used to but quit.

6. How many books have you read outside of school in the last year?
   a. None.
   b. 1 or 2.
   c. More than 2.

7. Which would you rather do?
   a. Work a job that requires you to work very few hours and just barely pays the rent.
   b. Work for free in an industry that you like.
   c. Get a high-paying job in an industry that you don't really like.

8. Are you considering more school after graduation?
   a. No thanks, I prefer the school of hard knocks.
   b. No way, thank heaven it's over.
   c. Yes, I might enroll in another program.

9. Why are you reading this book?
   a. It's an unexpected gift. I already have plans after graduation but was curious.
   b. It's an unexpected gift, and I have no plans after graduation.
   c. I bought this myself or asked for it as a gift.

10. A store is having an 80%-off sale. You think:
   a. I hate shopping.
   b. Cha-ching, it's my lucky day!
   c. I'll go and look around.

Scoring

Question	a	b	c	Your Score
1.	1	2	3	
2.	3	1	2	
3.	1	2	3	
4.	1	2	3	
5.	1	3	2	

6.	1	2	3	
7.	1	3	2	
8.	3	1	2	
9.	2	1	3	
10.	3	1	2	
Total Score:				

To score your quiz, write down the number corresponding to the letter of your answer for each question. For example, if you answered "a" for question 2, you would write 3 in the Your Score column for that question. Write down your score for each question and add the scores for all 10 questions for your Total Score. Write your Total Score somewhere and keep it handy. We will come back to this later when we start to examine your values, vision, and which way you are likely headed in life.

Short-Term vs. Long-Term Success

When you think about success, what things do you see? How would you know if you have become successful? How would you measure it? Success in life for most people involves achieving several individual goals. If all or most of those goals are achieved, we feel that we have generally succeeded. For the sake of simplicity we will break down success into two groups: short-term successes and long-term successes.

Short-term successes are goals that you have that are not part of a longer-range plan and that usually don't require a lot of time to achieve. Entertainment is an example of a short-term goal. Most people want to be entertained, and whatever form it comes in is usually easy to get and isn't part of a long-term plan. Surfing the Web for funny cat videos is entertaining and easy to do quickly, but fills no long-range need or plan. You are merely passing time as you amuse yourself. It feels good, sure, but it doesn't get you anywhere in the long run. It's a short-term success. Other examples of things that you might want to be successful at in the short term are satisfying hunger and avoiding confrontations.

Long-term successes are the things that you want that are enjoyed over a long span of time or are achieved in the more distant future. They are goals that take time, effort, and planning to achieve. Some of your long-term successes can be broken up into smaller parts, each of which you can achieve in a relatively short period of time. Still, those successes work together to build toward long-term success. Some examples of long-term successes are financial security, good family relationships, and good health. Eating healthy food and exercising every day will lead to good health over time. These concepts of short-term and long-term successes and how they can compete with each other will be covered again in the chapter about values and visions.

Be True

Perhaps the most difficult part of finding success is that your definition of it might change over time because you, as a person, change. You are influenced by the world around you and evolve over the time spent on your journey. Your thoughts and desires drift and alter with the circumstances and experiences of life. Some of your goals now might be irrelevant or even laughable 10 years from now. And that is totally fine. There are likely a few goals, your core desires for life, that will remain fairly steady — good health, happy children, a comfortable home, and a loving spouse. Which car you want or where you want to go on your dream vacation might change frequently, but the basics, your core desires, are usually pretty firm.

As you venture off into the next phase of your life, take a few minutes to really explore your desires. What would it take for you to feel successful? Think through the little exciting things as well as those basic, core needs. Are these all the same goals that you had 10 years ago? Five years ago? If not, what changed? And more importantly, do you know why you changed? As we will explore later, your core goals or measures of your personal success can take a back seat to your more volatile dreams. For example, you might want to be independently wealthy someday, but that shiny new car is calling your name—today. The cars come and go, and your needs and wants shift, but you likely will always desire financial security, if not real wealth.

THINK WHERE YOU'RE GOING

Take time every once in a while, maybe every new year or near your birthday, to think about your core goals for success and the goals that are likely to change. If you aren't making headway toward those core goals, ask yourself why. Are your near-term desires having an effect on your long-term success? Are you sacrificing your success at good health by trying to impress others with your cool, smoker look? Friends might come and go, but you only have one body for the rest of your life. Stay in tune with who you really are deep down inside and pay attention to those things that steer you in another direction. Being true to yourself requires constant vigilance and making any necessary adjustments to ensure that your core goals, those long-term successes, aren't jeopardized.

2

Categories

All mankind is divided into three groups:
those that are immovable, those that are movable
and those that move.
-Anonymous

Categories

Graduation from high school presents you with several choices. After college graduation, however, you have no choice but to enter the workforce. You will be thrust out into the world as an educated graduate. I am assuming that you are like most graduates in that you are not already wealthy, either through your own means or through your family. Therefore, starting now, you will need to begin to pay your way through the world. And again, many of you will have some form of loan to repay if you are graduating from a college of some sort. If you are a high school grad then you may have another few years of reprieve from "the real world" if you have your sights set on college or trade school.

Actually, you high school graduates that are headed for another few years of education have both an advantage and a disadvantage. Your advantage is that you have some time to figure out your success story or vision. You can hone in on your core needs and practice keeping them in your thoughts. You have the advantage of being able to tailor your education and experiences to give you the best chance of attaining success after graduation. Your disadvantage, as you college graduates can likely attest to, is that you face an unimaginable set of distractions and influences. If you aren't careful you could end up no better off in four years than you are right now. Maybe even worse. Your disadvantage is time or rather your perception of time. You may feel like you have more time than you really do to make decisions. Four years feels like a long time now, but once it is gone, it is gone. If you're graduating from college right now, today is the day you must take action. There is no more time for planning or procrastinating. Now is the time that you need to get a place to live, buy food, and live life. As you look back now, even at your young age, you might begin to see the importance and scarcity of time.

There are many types of people in the world and many ways to group them or categorize them. For example, we can group people by their nationality, hair color, gender, or by IQ level. How people think about and spend their time now, along with their present thoughts and actions, can also be a way to categorize people. In order to group people according to how they live their lives based on the choices that they make, we will create five groups or categories:

- Criminals
- Strugglers
- Idlers
- Workers
- Controllers

With the exception of the criminal group, there is nothing inherently good or bad about any of these categories, but you should know them and understand them. Whether you want to end up in any particular one or not, your thoughts and actions are placing you into one of these categories right now. If you find that you aren't where you want to be in life or aren't achieving your personal version of success, knowing how our society works will help you to make the shifts that you need to make in order to get where you want to be.

HIGHLIGHT: Whether you realize it or not, your thoughts and actions are already placing you into categories within society and defining your life's path.

Criminals are people who repeatedly and deliberately choose not to play by the rules of an ethical society. These include mob bosses and serial murderers. Strugglers are those people who, due to circumstances that are mostly beyond their control at the moment, cannot make rational decisions or choices for the long-term future. They are just struggling to survive. The remaining three categories of people, idlers, workers, and controllers, are the ones we focus on here. The people in these categories differ from one another in several important ways.

First, they differ in *how they view time*. They each treat their personal time differently in sometimes subtle, but very significant, ways. Second, they differ in *the goals or successes they focus on*. Some focus on their immediate success goals, and others focus more on their longer-term or core goals and successes. Lastly, they differ in *what they know about money (their financial literacy) and their attitudes toward money.*

Like many things in life, these categories are not black-and-white. You typically aren't in just one category and none of the others. The categories are presented here as individual groups to make the concepts clearer, but they are actually part of a spectrum of how people make choices. At one end of the spectrum are true idlers and at the other end are true controllers. Falling in the middle (that is, being in the workers category) means you have tendencies or some thought patterns and behaviors of both idlers and controllers, which is typical of most people. Your particular place on the spectrum is often not as important as your trajectory on the spectrum. Are you happy with your current state of affairs? Are you at least moving in the right direction to achieve what success means to you?

> **HIGHLIGHT:** Most people fall into the spectrum between extremes, the worker category, with tendencies towards either the idler or controller categories.

Let's explore each of the three groups briefly, but as we do so keep in mind that I am only trying to show you how things operate. It is up to you to make your own choices. Which category you end up in is up to you. As long as you are self-supporting and not negatively affecting others, there is no right or wrong group. There is only what is right for you personally.

Idlers

Idlers are commonly identified with youth and those who seek immediate, simple pleasures. Some people might call them slackers or couch potatoes. Again, I am not saying that idlers are bad. Indeed, I think they serve a purpose in our society. While some of them may truly be slackers or couch potatoes, these are not always accurate descriptions for idlers. Idlers could be very busy at something, but whatever they put their efforts into isn't moving them toward their long-term goals or successes. They could be very involved and active in their hobby or activity of choice, but the problem is that whatever they are doing isn't productive from a monetary or other long-term goal perspective. Idlers are primarily low-level consumers with little to no ambition or activity in pursuit of higher incomes or greater wealth. They might have desires, but there is no initiative or action. Idlers might have similar core or long-term goals as the other groups, but more often than not they allow their shorter-term successes to run their lives.

A seemingly odd thing about idlers is that they often value their time very highly. You may think that an idler doesn't place a high value on much of anything given their typically carefree lifestyle. In fact, they can be fiercely defensive of their personal time. Their immediate pleasures and short-term success goals might be impeded by full-time employment or other non-pleasure activities. They prefer to use their time directly for things that they enjoy doing in a one-for-one trade. One hour of their time is spent for one hour of online gaming fun, for example.

Money is often viewed as a necessary evil by those in this category and might even be actively avoided. Low financial literacy is typical, so they struggle to make money work for them. Money is spent as soon as it is made, and credit (if they can get it) is often used to maintain their lifestyle in the short term. Low income and subsistence living is the typical hallmark of idlers. They usually have a fair amount of personal time, which is grudgingly traded for income when needed to pay basic bills such as rent and food. Idlers can have only a limited impact on their financial standing due to low financial understanding and low leverage. I'll say more about leverage later, but basically idlers' time and effort cannot be amplified or replicated without the same amount of additional effort on their part. One hour of work gets one hour worth of reward and that's it. For example, if Tina works for one hour and gets $10, and then spends it all on dinner out after work and goes home, one hour of her time was completely spent for $10. Her money is gone so there is no way it can be used as a tool to get more income.

If spending as little time working as possible and enjoying your personal time, although with little money, sounds good to you, then an idler might be what you want to be. If you've read this far in the book, then you probably aren't idler material, though. An important point about idlers is that they are in this position by choice, not by circumstance. Being laid off from your job due to industry cutbacks might place you into the struggler group temporarily. Being fired from that job because you don't care probably will land you in the idler group. Given the amount of information and communication readily available at your fingertips today, it takes a conscious choice to choose the idler lifestyle and stick with it.

Workers

Workers make up a large group of people in our society. They are typically those with aspirations of achieving some of those fundamental, or long-term, success goals, such as financial security. However, they are often hindered and distracted by those pesky short-term successes, such as impressing the neighbors. People who are working in some form or another to gain income to pay their bills are usually in the workers category. People in this category, such as sales associates, engineers, and lawyers—like idlers—trade their time for money on a one-to-one basis.

Workers differ from idlers in that they, at least occasionally, have an eye on their future. Their longer-term goals rise to the top of their consciousness, and they put some effort toward achieving them. The worker goes to a job, gets paid, and uses that money for basic expenses, some leisure activities and recreation, as well as savings or investments. Savings accounts, 401(k) accounts, or even home buying are ways that they attempt to save and leverage their money for the future. The goals of workers are a mix of short-term and long-term successes. In our society this is a tough place to be mentally. The constant bombardment of advertisements and images of what you ought to be or ought to have is hard to ignore. The commercial systems of companies that are trying to sell you things are geared up and finely tuned to take advantage of the fact that idlers and workers can be easy targets. Achieving the long-term successes of health, wealth, fame, or happiness is hampered by all of these distractions.

Time is an element that the worker also struggles with. Workers see and acknowledge longer-term goals and make an attempt to attain them. Usually this involves following the path of a good education and/or a decent job. That decent job provides some amount of security and limited income. The income from the job is obtained by trading personal time for a set amount of money. Workers sell parts of their lives for money. This is just like the idler but normally on a larger scale.

Workers tend to work a lot. If they are salaried, which means they receive a fixed amount of money per year, then the more they work, the less they make on a per-hour basis. Two things happen here. The value of their working time drops, and the value of their personal time also drops. Let's say Tina graduates and gets a job making $45,000 per year. A standard 40-hour work week means she essentially makes $21.63 per hour. Tina works in a busy job and feels like she must work an extra hour per day to keep up with the workload or at least make herself look good to her boss. That extra hour per day drops her effective pay rate to $19.23 per hour. The value of her working time has dropped.

But wait, there's more. Tina's personal time every workday would probably be around five hours. If she wakes up at 6:00 a.m. and gets ready for work, commutes to work, works from 8:00 a.m. to 5:00 pm., heads home, and arrives there at 6:00 p.m., that leaves from 6:00 p.m. to 11:00 p.m. as her waking personal time. If she spends one extra hour working per workday, that means she is trading 20% of her personal time each workday for nothing. Tina has lowered the value of her personal time by willingly giving it away and lowered the cash value of her working time. There might, however, be some instances where this pans out a little better in the long run. If Tina's extra work lands her a raise, promotion, bonus, or similar benefit, perhaps it was a good short-term trade off. That is up to Tina to decide.

Helpful Info: Comparing being paid hourly to being paid a salary
- A standard work week is 40 hours.
- A standard work year is 2080 hours.
- Divide an annual salary by 2080 to get the per-hour equivalent.
- Many hourly positions pay lower on a per-hour basis compared to salary, with the expectation of paid overtime providing the difference.

So far, workers are just like idlers. They trade their time, the seconds of their lives, for a fixed amount of money. It may be a little more or a little less, as in Tina's case. The difference comes into play when they think about the money that they have earned. The idler thinks no further than spending. Buy what you want and what you need right now and look no further. Got an extra 50 bucks? Buy that new video game. Bam! Done. The worker, however, might realize that saving some of that money is probably a good idea. Who knows what the future holds? You might have visions or plans that you know of, and there are certainly things that will happen that you didn't expect or plan for—planning for a rainy day, as the saying goes. How workers save their money will take several forms, and we'll cover those in a bit. How much they know about money and how it works, as well as their attitude toward money, will dictate what they do with that extra money. The worker category has a wide range of financial literacy, whereas the idler category typically has a very small range of financial literacy.

The worker category is for you if you desire to work for income and then save and invest a portion of that income for a modest amount of security and comfort. There's no harm in that at all, but you likely won't become wealthy in either money or time very quickly. Your time will mostly be controlled by other people, because you are part of a system that needs you to perform your tasks. Whether you are a high-level manager, a machinist, or run your own small bakery, your time is traded for money on a one-for-one basis. Most workers are in the middle class. There are always exceptions, of course, such as very high-paid doctors, lawyers, or professional sports figures. These people still work for their money, but their hourly pay rate is off the charts. They might make a lot of money, but if they stop working the money flow stops, just as it does for the rest of the workers.

Controllers

Controllers refer to people who control their own destinies to the greatest extent possible. Controllers have a plan, and they make choices that are in line with that plan. They make decisions and take actions to propel themselves down their chosen road of success. Focusing primarily on long-term goals, sometimes to an extreme degree, is a hallmark of controllers. They know what they want out of life, and they don't give up control to somebody else with the expectation that the other person will make good things happen. Depending on their definition of success, many of them will need to control systems in order to leverage their time, talents, and money. Systems can be any process that has been created to produce a desired result. Companies are common examples of systems that are created to produce goods or services in exchange for profit. A simpler example is an automatic lawn sprinkler system which saves the owner time that he would have spent watering the lawn himself. Both of these things provide benefits to the owner or user after they have spent the initial effort to create them.

Being controllers does not necessarily mean that they are overbearing and unpleasant. However, they might be both of those things, and you might know of a few controllers who exhibit both traits. Unlike workers who only work as part of a system, controllers create, run, and benefit from the systems with which they are associated. They control them. Businesses are systems that create value by doing things like selling products for money. Business owners and investors create the system and reap the rewards that come from it in the form of profits.

The key to understanding controllers is the notion of gaining income without spending equal—or any—time on a particular activity. At a minimum, controllers don't trade their time for income in a one-for-one manner in the same way idlers and workers do. Controllers put in time up front to create a system that will provide benefits, value, or money with either reduced effort on their part or greatly magnified returns on their effort once the system is up and running. Doing this often requires a greater focus on those long-term successes or goals. Where do you want to be in five years or 10 years? It takes commitment to forgo more of the short-term successes and work toward those that are further out and harder to reach. Should Tom spend $30 to go out on a Thursday evening or use that money to buy a book on website coding and work on a website idea or a phone app? That choice might seem easy and inconsequential in the moment, but it could have ripple effects for years to come.

How you think about money and the choices that you make with your time are habits, and habits are hard to break once they have formed. You've probably been honing your current habits for years, whether you were aware of them or not. To make matters worse, a large part of our society is geared toward keeping you addicted to your "bad" habits. Easy credit, fast-food, and sexy men and women in advertisements are all designed to get your money by focusing on your short-term goals. Sure, who doesn't want to feel sexy or cool? Who wants to feel like an outsider because they stayed home or bought the inexpensive used car instead of the new sports car, you know, the one you've had your eye on? Just like procrastinating on your homework felt good in the short term, always picking the short-term goal will satisfy you in the moment but will eventually lead to a place that you probably would rather not be.

CATEGORIES

Controllers have a different attitude toward time than do people in the other categories. Controllers value their personal time very highly, as do idlers. They value it so highly, in fact, that they will do almost anything in the short term to gain their long-term personal time or have the ability to multiply its value greatly. Workers do this as well, but since they don't value their personal time as highly, they trade more of it earlier in time for lots of it later on. Think about it. If you spend 40 or 50 years working at a job with evenings and weekends free so that you can then retire and have all of your personal time when you are old, then you are a worker. Spending five years of all of your personal time creating a system that lets you enjoy the following 60 years of personal time makes you a controller.

Gaining that leverage, creating that system or company, and understanding the future requires a solid financial literacy. The odds of success are in your favor if you choose to try to become a controller, because most of your competition in life probably isn't going to pick up a book after graduation. The top 1% of our society in terms of income or wealth are often used as a comparison point or benchmark. Who are the 1% or even the 5% and how did they get into that group? Are they just lucky, or did they do something different? A little effort now might go a long way toward helping you realize your dreams.

Time is the Key

The descriptions of idlers, workers, and controllers might have given you the idea that time is a big player. Time is the major characteristic that defines these three groups of people. Your attitude about time—how you spend it and how you value it—will define your category and to a large extent your path in life.

> **HIGHLIGHT:** Much of your life's path will be determined by how you view and value your time.

Idlers care about their personal time but make little effort to change how their personal time is spent or the amount of personal time that they have. Idlers work as required to get just enough money to get by—and no more. In their mind, the small portion of the world that they experience in their daily lives is enough, and sometimes too much for them. They have little interest in exploring the possibilities outside of what they already know.

With respect to time, workers do two things. First, they trade more of their personal time by working more hours in an effort to improve the quality of what little personal time is then left for them. The extra income generated allows weekends and vacations to be more enjoyable. Second, they trade time now and throughout much of their life in order to gain more personal time near the end of their life. Many years are traded for the ultimate weekend known as retirement. Those years are traded at a fairly low rate of return. Those 40, 50, or 60 hours every week are traded for a finite amount of money, a few hours each day, and two whole days per week if they're lucky. Very little leverage is used by the worker to improve his or her situation. By leverage I mean finding a way to get more from your time or money without more effort. Stock investments or 401(k) accounts, for example, are ways to leverage your money. There's more on that coming up.

Controllers, on the other hand, control not only a system but their time as well. They are much more careful than idlers and workers are about how their time is spent. Controllers create systems that are designed to do one thing and one thing only: make value, most often in the form of money, without having to spend their time doing it. Imagine that. If you could create and build a machine that printed money whether you were there turning the handle or not, what could you do with your time? Controllers spend their time up front actually creating "machines" that make money so that they can have as much personal time as possible to spend the way they want to.

Of the many resources in the world—money, oil, gold, water, steel, and diamonds, for example—time is the only one that cannot be transferred to somebody else. We each have 24 hours in each day. Money is abundant in many places on this planet. It is all around you and fairly easy to get more of by trading your time, selling your possessions or in some cases simply asking for some. Time, however, is not like that. You have a limited number of hours each day, and no amount of money or effort can change that. It's up to you to use those hours wisely.

HIGHLIGHT: Time is a scarce resource that, unlike money, cannot be transferred or increased.

Comparisons

Idlers, workers, and controllers are just categories of people with different views of the world. There are pros and cons for each group, and your selection of which group you want to be in is up to you. Each group is differentiated from the others through a combination of how they think and spend their time regarding three key areas. Those areas are how they focus on short-term versus long-term goals, how they value their time, and how much they understand about money and wealth. The differences can be shown visually in the following three figures.

Figure 2.1 shows how each group focuses on its goals. Idlers focus mainly on short-term successes such as satisfying their need for entertainment. Controllers, on the opposite side of the chart, focus primarily on their longer-term successes. Workers occupy a wide range in the middle, with varying degrees of focus on each type of success. They focus on both, but can easily slide left and right on the scale on an almost daily basis.

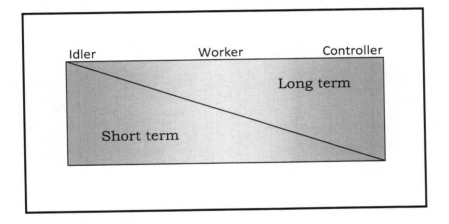

Figure 2.1: Focus Length

How members of each group value their time is shown in Figure 2.2. Idlers, on the left, place a fairly high value on their personal time and avoid activities that might consume that time in the short term. As one moves over toward the worker area, the value placed on personal time falls off and is replaced by other values. Controllers often place the highest value on time. This value of time might be shown in the form of doing activities that gain personal time, or it might be shown by how they leverage their time.

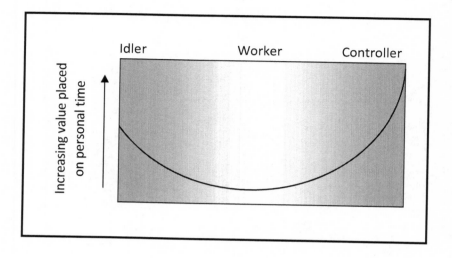

Figure 2.2: Time Value

Figure 2.3 shows the level of financial literacy generally required to be in each group. Financial literacy is how much you know about money and how to make it work for you. Idlers can have a very low level of financial literacy and a low level of interest in it. This combination can lead them to make dubious choices regarding financial deals that seem too good to be true. Controllers use their knowledge of money and time to achieve their goals and successes. Workers, of course, are in the middle group that is still learning about money systems, or they have quit learning altogether and are no longer advancing.

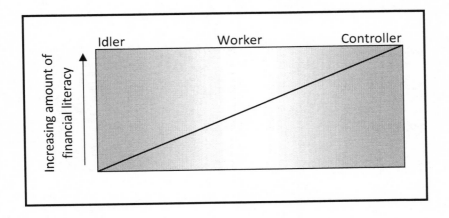

Figure 2.3: Financial Literacy

There is one more point that needs to be made clear. Being an idler, worker, or controller does not automatically make you rich or poor. While idlers might tend to be poor, and controllers might tend to be rich, the worker group spans the entire spectrum. There are plenty of workers who work very hard and are still poor. There are also many workers who work hard and gain some level of financial success or become "rich." Remember, having lots of money does not necessarily mean that you are successful, unless that was your ultimate goal.

THINK WHERE YOU'RE GOING

3

Money

A little knowledge is a dangerous thing.
-English proverb

What is Money?

I've talked about money quite a bit so far. It's not that money should be your obsession or primary focus. It's just that it is an important tool in your life that should be understood. So what is money? Is it a dollar? That's one type of it. Money is the thing we use to conveniently trade value. Trading and bartering directly with others works fairly well as long as both parties have what the other party wants. If Tina has a car that she doesn't want, and Tom has a diamond ring that he doesn't want, then perhaps they can just trade. But what if Tom doesn't want the car, but Ted does. Let's say Ted is offering up some of his time and talent as a painter. Tina could use a painter but would have to need a lot of painting to equal the value of the car. You see how this gets complicated quickly.

How about if Tina, Tom, Ted, and everyone in their town agrees that they will print some paper tokens of a set value? One token equals one hour of painting, for example. As long as they all agree that those tokens have a given amount of value, they can begin to exchange them in place of actual things. Tina gives Ted one token for one hour of painting. Tina got that token because she traded her car to Tom for 2,000 tokens, and Tom had traded something of his for the tokens he gave Tina. That is the basics of money. It is just a lot easier to carry tokens, or money, in your pocket than lugging around a big bag of everything that you wish to trade.

Money works because we all agree that it works. The U.S. dollar and many other world currencies were based on gold instead of one hour of painting as in the example. As long as we all agreed that gold was valuable, then all was well. Today, the dollar is not really backed by anything other than our collective agreement that is has a certain value to us.

Why Is Money Important?

Money is important because it simplifies and speeds up transactions. It also allows us to reach into the future, for better or for worse. We can easily combine our money with other people's money to do things that we couldn't do on our own. Money is a very powerful tool and one that will elude you or bite you if you don't pay some attention to it and learn about it.

Money doesn't make the world go around—just modern society. Money is a fascinating and powerful tool that is available to you to use as you please. Pursue your dreams, help your fellow mankind, or do nothing. The choice is yours, and money is what lets you do that. Even if you have no desire to be rich, but only want to help your fellow man, how much could you do with $5? With $5,000? With $5 million? Even $5 can make a difference.

> **HIGHLIGHT**: Money is merely a tool. It can help you if used carefully or hurt you if used carelessly.

In its simplest form, money provides important items like food, shelter, and health care in exchange for some of your time. In its most complex forms, it can be used as a tool to focus resources, power, and time to achieve amazing things much faster than would ever be possible without it.

History of Money

Thousands of years ago, the early societies used barter, gifting, and debt to operate. Barter is simply trading. Want a goat? I'll trade you three chickens for it. Most interactions occurred between people who knew one another in their local area, since travel and communication were rather slow affairs. The first use of commodity money, called tokens in our example above and known as shekels, is thought to have come from Mesopotamia around 3000 BC. Mesopotamia covered parts of what are now Syria, Iraq, and Kuwait. The shekel was a gold or silver coin that stood for a certain weight, sometimes of barley. Over time, other things were used to back money, such as cowry shells or gold. Money is typically backed by something that is both somewhat scarce and valued in the society. You wouldn't want to use dirt to back your money because everyone could get more of it and inflation would be off the charts, making the money almost worthless.

The first actual minted or stamped coins to be used as money are believed to have come from the Lydians around 600 BC. Paper money showed up in China around 1000 AD, and the idea made its way to Europe in the 13th century. These notes were originally just receipts or IOUs and didn't hold actual value. After a while the paper became an accepted way to buy things without having to convert the paper back into gold. Paper notes backed up by predetermined quantities of gold were standard in Europe by the 19th century.

By the end of World War II, most countries were fixing their currency to the U.S. dollar, which was backed by gold. In the early days you could convert your paper dollars into gold, but that was done away with in the 1970s. This action naturally caused a bit of displeasure around the world, and many countries stopped basing the value of their currency on the U.S. dollar.

Good Things about Money

Let's talk about what is good about money. A bit of this has been touched on already. Money makes transactions easier between everyone in a society. There's no more hauling around a cage full of chickens when you go shopping to trade for a new shirt. I mentioned earlier that money allows you to reach into the future, for better or for worse. How is that possible?

If you are a worker, as are most people, you might desire to own a nice house of your own to live in. You have two choices for that to happen. First, you can save up all of the extra money that you can and buy the house with cash when you are able to afford it. If you save $10,000 a year, it will take you 15 years to buy a $150,000 house, give or take. If you don't want to wait that long, you can get a loan, called a mortgage, to buy the house right now. What you are essentially doing when you get a mortgage is trading a whole bunch of your future time for the money you get now so that you can buy the house you want. Do you want to go skiing on a Tuesday next month? Sorry, that time is already booked and no longer available to you because you bought a house with a loan. You must spend that time working to earn the money that you agreed to pay back.

This is exactly where people tend to get into trouble. Using money to leverage or use your future means that you are guessing about the future. You are assuming that you will still be able to pay down that loan next year, in five years, and 20 years from now. You are assuming that you will actually still want that house in five years. Sure, you can sell it, but that costs money and time, and it comes with the assumption that somebody else will pay enough for it so you don't lose money in the process.

Buying a house with a loan is a big example, but the same thing applies on a smaller scale. Take credit cards, for example. A credit card is just a flexible loan with nothing securing it. I'll go over some of this financial terminology in a minute, but for now just treat the credit card as a small loan. If you whipped out your credit card to buy a fantastic dress or new baseball hat, you bought it with a loan. Remember that a loan often means you are paying for it with your future, not with cash that you already earned in the past. The problem with using your future to pay for things now is that it narrows your options or choices. Worse than that, it drastically lowers the value of your time. Here's how.

Buying things on credit or with a loan can often lead to a multiplying problem. If you buy a dress on credit today because you wouldn't have the cash until next week, guess what happens next week? If your car breaks down, you can't pay cash to fix it because you don't have any (but you do have that awesome dress), and you won't have any next week either because that money has to pay for the dress. So for the next two to three weeks all of your money is spoken for. You have no options but to keep working to get the money to pay off the debts. If this pattern of using credit continues for very long, you are looking at an extended period of time needed to work to pay off all of the things that you bought when you didn't have cash. Your future is used up before you even get there. For many workers and idlers, the cycle of getting a job, going to work, paying your monthly credit card bill, and repeating goes on for 50 years or more.

Not all loans and other forms of credit will cause a person to enter that unpleasant cycle, though. The reason for this is that controllers use the money they obtain through loans and other credit differently than workers do. Workers normally get loans and use credit to buy things that they *want* but can't pay cash for, such as cars, houses, TVs, clothes, and so forth. But controllers use loans and credit to get things that they *need*. They use them as tools to help build their systems. When they do use credit to buy things that they want, they do it very deliberately to either control costs, taxes, or cash flow. They typically don't do it because they couldn't afford something. I see that we are starting to get close to the topics of making money, controlling costs, and the like at this point. Before we get into too much of that, let's make sure we have a common language and understanding of the terms.

Terms

This book isn't intended to be a complete financial or investment guide, so we will only briefly cover a few basic terms here that will help you as you get started and aid in our discussions. There are many other books and resources available for obtaining more in-depth information on any of these topics.

Loan

A loan is when somebody gives you a bunch of money up front that you have to repay later. You can either repay it all at once or a little at a time, in what are called installments. Large or risky loans usually have collateral to secure them.

Collateral

When you borrow money from somebody, the lender is taking the risk that you might not pay the loan back. To make sure the lender gets all or most of the money back you might be asked to offer something to the lender that he or she can have if you can't pay off the loan. For a loan on a house (a mortgage), the house itself is the collateral. If you can't make the payments, the bank takes ownership of the house, kicks you out, and sells the house. The same thing happens with a car loan. If you don't make the car payments, the lender can repossess the car.

Credit

Credit is like a loan, but normally without collateral and it usually isn't given all at once. The amount of credit you have is set at the beginning. A credit card with a $1,000 limit means you can spend up to $1,000 any way you want to. You sign an agreement with the bank or provider giving you credit that defines how and when you have to repay the money and what the service will cost you. That cost is typically called interest, but there can be other costs and fees as well.

Interest

The cost of borrowing money is usually calculated as a percentage of the money that you owe and is called interest. The interest rate is that percentage which is charged to you at certain intervals of time such as each week, month or year.

Mortgage

A loan taken out to buy a house is called a mortgage and uses the house as collateral. If your house is worth more than you owe on it you can take out another loan or second mortgage that is secured by that equity or value. Mortgages, like most loans, require you to pay interest on the amount that you owe to the lender.

Equity

The value of something after you deduct what you still owe on it is your equity. For example, if you own a car worth $9,000 and you still owe $3,500, your equity is $5,500.

Leverage

"Leverage" in a money sense is similar to its meaning in a physical sense. If you use a pry bar to pull out a nail from a wall or a piece of wood, you are using leverage by applying force in one place and seeing a greater force in another location. Leverage increases your advantage so that you have to do less work to get the results that you want. For money, the same effect as the pry bar can be very powerful and very dangerous. A credit card or loan allows you to leverage your future or focus it to buy things now. They are tools that focus your future efforts into actions that you will take today. Leverage can also mean using tools or other people, like employees, to your benefit.

Speculation

"Speculation" is another way to say "gambling" or "guessing." If you speculate in real estate, it means that you are likely buying properties with the hope or expectation that their value will go up, without your having any special knowledge or reason for thinking the value will increase. The value might go down, because you don't really know what the market will do in the future.

Investing

Putting your money or time to work, or buying something that will become more valuable over time, is called investing. You can invest your time in studying and practicing to become an actor with the intent that someday you will be a highly paid movie star. You can invest your money in the stock market with the expectation that what you buy now will be worth more next month, next year, or in future years. Investing is usually associated with some kind of managed risk and educated assumptions. If you blindly buy something that you know nothing about in the hope that it becomes more valuable, that's not really investing, it's just guessing or speculating.

Stocks

When a company wants to raise money, one of its options is to sell off small portions of ownership of the company to other people. These little percentages of ownership are called stock. If you buy stock in Ford

Motor Company, you are an owner of that company. You are one of many owners, of course, but you are still an owner. One downside of a company creating stock is the possible loss of full control of the business.

Bonds

Bonds are loans that you, as an individual, make to a government or company that promises to pay you back with some interest. Bonds are typically a safer way to make some profit than stocks, but the amount of profit is set at the start. Even if the stock market goes up like a rocket, your bond will only earn you the yearly percentage that was negotiated or fixed when you bought the bond.

Funds

A group of people who pool their money to buy investments can create a fund. A fund is managed by a professional so that individual participants in the fund don't have to deal with its operations. Funds are usually focused on a certain type of investment or stock, or they use a strategy to achieve a certain goal. A large-cap fund will focus on companies with the highest market capitalization, while a 30-year retirement fund will try to maximize the values at a time farther in the future, when you expect to need the money.

401(k)

Many types of retirement savings and investment methods are available today, but one of the more

66

common ones that you are likely to hear about is a 401(k). A 401(k) account is a way to invest part of your paycheck before you pay taxes on it. So instead of only putting $8 dollars in after taxes have been withheld, you get to put in $10 before taxes, for example. One advantage is that this higher amount of money invested early might grow faster. A second advantage is that the taxes you pay now are lowered. Another benefit that you might find is that your employer might throw a little extra money in. This is called a match. If they equally match up to 5%, that means that if you put in 5% of your check, they will put in the same amount as an extra bonus. Free money! You do have to pay taxes when you take the money out of the investment, but your tax bracket and associated tax rate might be lower in retirement than during your working career. If you want to take some money out of your account before you retire, you can do so, but there is often a stiff monetary penalty.

Market

A market is just a place where people make transactions. The stock market is the system in which people can buy and sell stocks, just like a farmers' market is where you can buy and sell vegetables.

When people refer to market share or whether there is a market for a certain product, they are referring to demand. Demand from the general public for a certain thing is called the market for that item. If 10 million cars were sold in the United States last year, the market for cars is 10 million or a little more. Offering a new product for sale that nobody buys means that there probably isn't a market for it.

Compound Interest

Taking the money you have made in the form of interest and adding that back into the original investment is a way to speed up the rate at which you make money. That's what compound interest is. The interest that you earn is added to your balance and continues to earn additional interest itself. It can be a very powerful tool over the long run as the interest builds upon itself.

Inflation

Inflation is the gradual increase in the price of things. Another way to say it is that money, or a single dollar, slowly loses value over time. A simple example of inflation: A candy bar cost $0.10 in 1950 and $1.50 in 2015. It is essentially the same candy bar that is made the same way, but a dollar is not as valuable as it was 65 years ago due to inflation. The reasons for inflation are varied and are the topic of much research and debate. You can find lots of information about that research elsewhere if you are interested. Deflation is the opposite of inflation and occurs when prices begin to drop. Such a price move often occurs when an economy slows down dramatically.

4

Using Money

A fool and his money are soon parted.
-Proverb

Loans and Credit

The ability to leverage your future with loans and credit is a powerful thing. This power can be used to your benefit, but can also get you into a lot of trouble. In the Terms section in the previous chapter, we covered a few words that you might commonly hear, such as interest, mortgage, and equity. Before you run out and buy a new car with your graduation gift money, let's take a minute to understand what is happening and what you will really be paying if you do that.

As we said, a loan or credit means that somebody has given you money that you have agreed to pay back either over time or all at once sometime in the future. This service almost always comes with a price, and that price is the interest. There might be other fees associated with the loan, but let's focus on the interest for now. You are paying the bank a fee so that it will help you buy the car now. When you ask for a loan to buy something, you will be offered the terms of the loan. The terms of the loan include how long you have to pay it back, when and how often you will make payments, what the interest rate is, and what, if any, up-front costs or fees there are. Let's walk through an example.

Tim walks into the car dealership and finds the perfect shiny black pickup truck. What a great way to start his new life after graduation, right? A new chapter with some new wheels! The sticker price or posted price of the truck is $35,000. With some rebates from the manufacturer and a little negotiating between Tim and the salesman, the final price of the truck is $31,250. Tim doesn't have much cash (he just graduated last week), so he asks for a loan for the full price of the truck.

The woman responsible for financing cars and trucks at the dealership sits down with Tim and offers him a loan through a bank with the following terms:

Sale price: $31,250
Sales tax: $2,000
Registration fees: $200
Origination fee: $500
Down payment: $0
Amount financed: $33,950
Annual interest rate: 6%
Loan term: 60 months
Payments: Monthly on the 10th of each month
Monthly payment amount: $656.35

Sounds okay, right? It's a brand-new truck for $656 per month. Let's say that was you and not Tim. If you pay off the truck by making that monthly payment for five years, you will have paid $39,381 in total for the truck. Wait, what? That's $5,431 dollars more than what the loan amount was in the beginning. That money, thanks to the 6% interest rate, is what you pay to be able to borrow the money from the bank and is paid back in little amounts from every monthly payment that you make. That monthly interest or finance charge is typically higher at the beginning and lower at the end of the loan term. The following chart shows what the monthly payment would be and how much interest you would pay for the same truck given different interest rates, but keeping everything else the same.

Rate	Monthly Payment	Total Interest Paid
4%	$625.24	$3,564.40
6%	$656.35	$5,431.00
8%	$688.38	$7,352.80
10%	$721.34	$9,330.40

Figure 4.1: Auto Loan Interest Example

You can easily find any number of websites that will help you calculate these types of numbers for any kind of loan that you're considering.

So the loan terms offered above are kind of a bummer, right? You'll have to pay an extra five grand. Suppose that you decide to go for it, feeling that the $656 a month payment and the insurance bill are within your budget given your new job offer. You tell yourself that you can always just sell the truck if you get into trouble, too. Hold on, that might not work out so well for you. You see, the second you drive that truck off the lot it is no longer new and begins to lose value. Cars and trucks lose value pretty quickly at first, but that rate of loss eases up a little toward the end of their life. Most vehicles are considered to have little to no value between 10 and 15 years of age. In the early part of your ownership of that shiny new truck, it is losing value faster than you are paying it off. At the end of two years, it might be worth about $18,000, but you will still owe $21,026. If you lost your job and had to sell that truck you would lose over three grand.

Loans on items that lose value (that depreciate), can put you in a tough spot if you don't maintain enough cash or other assets to cover them. Credit cards can be even worse. Credit cards can have much higher interest rates, especially for the young or others with poor or short credit histories. Interest rates on cards can easily be over 20%. High rates, combined with the practice of allowing you to make minimum payments, will cost you a lot in the end and can really jeopardize the availability of future choices for you.

Imagine that Tina gets a new credit card with a $5,000 limit (the most she can charge) with a 15% interest rate. In a brilliant flash of excitement, she goes on a post-graduation shopping spree and maxes out that card. She buys clothes, shoes, jewelry, a new TV, dinner for her friends, and a much needed trip to Mexico. When her bill arrives, it shows that she owes $5,000. Ouch. Scanning down the page she sees that she only has to pay the minimum payment of $112.50. That doesn't seem so bad, right? She should easily be able to pay that this month. Let's look at this a bit closer though. That $112.50 is actually only paying the interest that she owes the bank. She is paying them that amount as a fee to borrow the money every month. If she just makes that minimum payment, she might *never* pay off the credit card. She will just keep paying the bank month after month after month and the balance will never go down. How long would you want to do that? Banks and similar companies make a lot of money. They make a lot of that money from you and me through interest charges, among other things.

All of this talk about loans and credit can seem a little depressing when you consider how much extra you can end up paying for purchases financed by those methods. For things that you buy that lose value, which is most things, this is part of the problem that many people get into. You pay more, can get in over your head, and have to pay for a long time, sacrificing your future personal time. These things that lose value are called depreciating assets. They depreciate (lose value) over time. There is another class of things called appreciating assets. These appreciating assets increase in value over time. When you buy things that appreciate or grow in value, you are investing in them. Is a car an investment? Not likely, because unless you bought a rare Ferrari, the car will lose value and only cost you money.

Idlers and workers spend most of their money on depreciating assets. The money is spent, and the value slowly fades away. If a loan or credit was used, idlers and workers spend even more money for the item in the long run and have to give up some of their future for it, not just their past. Controllers, on the other hand, try to spend their money first on appreciating assets, things that grow in value or make money. Only later do they spend it on depreciating assets. Buying appreciating assets first is how controllers create the systems that will provide them with money without a one-for-one time trade for it. To be clear, though, controllers will still use loans and credit, but they just use them differently, as we will see later.

Idlers usually don't buy appreciating assets. They usually don't invest, either. They earn money and spend it without thought for the future. This works fine as long as you are able to keep working as needed and your expenses don't change much. If you like what you do and where you are and aren't planning for anything different after you are 60 years old, then by all means have fun as an idler.

Workers are part idler and part controller. They earn money, spend most of it on depreciating things, and only spend a little on investments or appreciating assets. As a worker's wage increases, he or she often enters into a cycle of additional spending as a personal reward, followed by more work to keep up with the new expenses. Let's say that you get a job right after graduation, work hard all year long, and at the end of a year you get a raise. After a long, grueling year of 10-hour days being the new staff member, you probably will feel like you deserve a little reward. Your old car from college is falling apart and is by far the worst-looking vehicle in the parking lot. It certainly isn't helping much on the dating scene either. So why not get a new car? If you get a raise, it will pretty much cover the payment, so there's no harm in buying a new car now, right? After the car, there's a better place to live, a new TV so your new friends can come over and watch the game, and on and on. Welcome to the rat race. You have officially started. Good luck finding the finish line. The finish line is commonly believed to lie some 45 years in the future at retirement, when your 401(k), a couple of other stock buys, Social Security, and your home will hopefully keep you in high style for the next 30 years as your health fades away.

Controllers take a different approach. Valuing time as much as they do, they despise working to earn a wage to buy depreciating assets. That is a one-for-one (or worse) trade of their time. Instead, controllers will work tirelessly in the beginning to buy assets and create systems that will increase in value without much further effort. They are trying to gain both time and money. Leverage in the form of loans and credit are tools used by these people to gain more power early in the process. Instead of leveraging their own future time, they use other people's time and money to get ahead.

An example of this type of approach is home buying. Workers will likely have a strong desire at some point to stop renting and buy their own homes. When that time comes, do you think they will buy the cheapest house available or the most expensive one that they think they can make the payments on? A home is an investment, right? Well, it might not be, financially speaking. A lot of things come into play here, such as interest rates, the rate at which the house is gaining value, the type and length of loan that you have, and so on. It can be that homeowners are losing more money in taxes, interest payments, and maintenance than they are gaining from the home price appreciation. This is especially true early in the loan when the interest payment is much higher on a monthly basis. Figure 4.2 shows that in the beginning of the loan term, over 70% of your payment goes toward interest and is lost to you forever. The amount actually being used to pay off the house is called principal.

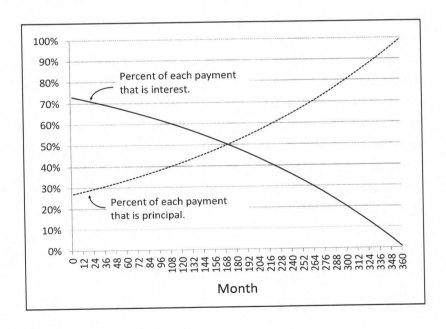

Figure 4.2: Payment Breakdown for 30-Year Home Loan

You would have to live in that home for quite some time to just break even when you sell it, unless you are in a super-hot market where prices are rising very rapidly.

Instead of buying a home right off the bat as an "investment," a controller is more likely to find some way to minimize that cost or eliminate it by leveraging somebody else. The first home I ever purchased was a duplex, and I rented out half of it to help cover my costs. I was young and single, and knew that I didn't need a full home and didn't want to pay full rent. My renters covered around 75% of my expenses, leaving me with a decent place to live and control over who I shared the building with. I also benefited from the increase in the value of the property due to a rising market. Controllers realize that unless something is providing money or cash flow every month or clearly increasing in net value, it is not an investment. Homes often fall into the latter category.

This is not to say that you shouldn't buy a home. But you need to examine all of the factors that go into that decision, such as:

- How much would you pay on a monthly basis compared to renting?
- How long are you planning to live in the house?
- Are property values expected to rise? Why? What is happening to the area or town that would cause that?

- Do you have any concerns such as children and schools that make owning a home in a certain neighborhood better than owning a home in another neighborhood?
- Could you efficiently add extra value to the home while you lived there?
- Which is better for your mental health and well-being, owning or renting?
- Can you buy a decent home that doesn't overextend you (one that you can easily afford)?

Affordable

Affordability has different meanings to different people, and so it's no surprise that idlers, workers, and controllers have different definitions of the word as well. The most frequently used and broad definition says that affordability is whether or not you can pay for something. Okay, that makes sense. If you can't actually pay for something, clearly you can't afford it. But is that all there is to it? Of course not. Like many things in life, as you are learning, there are subtleties that can have big impacts.

Idlers consider affordability to be whether or not they have the cash to outright pay for something or if they can make the minimum monthly payment using a credit card or a loan. They typically only think about this definition: Can they actually pay for it? The details and consequences of how they do it don't matter much.

Workers are bit more sophisticated when it comes to affordability. They often internally struggle over whether buying the item is a response to a want or whether it's a response to a true need. If they really want something, they might lean more toward the idler way of thinking. Buying a cool new phone would only cost $35 a month. Easy, right? Sure, you can come up with $35 a month. Bigger purchases tend to make them pause a little, though, and consider the broader picture. Even if they could afford to pay cash or make the payments, large expenditures are reviewed for longer-term impacts. They might feel a need to bolster their savings account for a rainy day instead of blowing it on a trip to Las Vegas. Perhaps a small windfall will make its way into a stock investment or college fund instead of a new TV. Affordability for these people depends partly on their vision for success and partly on their state of mind at the time of the decision, even if their finances say differently.

HIGHLIGHT: Affordable means different things to different people. Nothing can be said to be affordable without knowing the circumstances of the person buying it.

For controllers, affordability is pretty clear-cut. If they can't pay for something easily, with little to no negative impact on their future or current plans, it is not affordable. Credit is used only as a tool of either convenience for some reason or as a means of taking advantage of the nuances of credit deals in order to save money. For example, let's say you have an extra $5,000 that you don't need somewhere else, and you can easily spend it without any real impact on your finances. You see a hot tub that you want, and you talk to the salesperson about it. You learn that there is a special deal going on that would allow you to buy the hot tub on credit with no payments or interest for one year. Workers might see that deal and think that it is great because they can put off paying for it for a whole year. Maybe they even plan to spend the five grand on something else right away and then save up money over the year to help make the payments on the hot tub. Maybe they'd make a trip to Las Vegas now and just make the payments later. Either way, it's basically a free hot tub for the first year, right?

Controllers see this deal differently. They might buy the hot tub using the credit deal and invest the extra $5,000 they hold in cash for the year. When the time comes for the first payment on the hot tub, they might pay off the whole thing all at once. What does that do for them? First, let's say they earned an 8% return on that $5,000 investment for the year, which gave them an extra $400. Let's also assume that inflation for the year was 2%, meaning that, in general, at the end of the year the money they had was worth 2% less. By paying the whole amount for the tub one year later, the controller is using tomorrow's dollars to pay for today's prices. Dollars in the future are worth less than they are today. In one year, for example, that five grand would lose another $100 in value, or purchasing power. In the final accounting for the transaction, the controller would save about $500 by investing the money and paying the tub off later.

An extreme way to think about this concept is to consider a car in 1965. If you could have had a new car in 1965 that was worth $3,500, but you didn't have to pay that $3,500 until today, would you have done it? In today's market, $3,500 is much less valuable than it was in 1965. In other words, you would have an easier time of obtaining that amount today than you would have in 1965. An important point about how controllers would proceed in the hot tub example is this: Although they did use credit and paid in the future, they did not leverage their future time. The money was there the entire time, so they kept all of their options available. At any moment they could have paid off the hot tub and removed the debt. They used credit as a tool to make the item cheaper, not more expensive, which is what idlers or workers would have most likely done.

5

Income and Systems

Half the work, twice the effect.
-Chinese idiom

Income

If you live in a modern society and aren't independently wealthy, you are going to need to earn money in some way. Money that you earn is called income. Most people agree that there are two basic types of income: active and passive.

Active

Active income is the favored type of idlers and the most common type for workers. Active income is income that you have to actively work for. You have to trade your time, usually one-for-one, in exchange for payment. Hourly wages and salaries are typical, but even the self-employed and small business owners can have primarily active income.

A one-for-one active income is what hourly workers get. One hour of their time is traded for a fixed amount of money. To get more money, hourly workers have to merely work more hours. Simple. Salaried workers, on the other hand, get a one-for-one trade also, but their situation can be worse, because they receive no pay at all for hours they work in addition to the standard weekly number of hours. In some cases, working without pay might help in the long run with a raise or promotion, but in a typical situation it just devalues workers' time and doesn't provide them with any benefits. Some people might argue that salaried workers have more flexibility in that they get a fixed payment and don't have to be at work all the time.

That's true in some cases. As a salaried worker you might be able to run out of the office from time to time, but in my experience you are probably going to put in more work time than you get back in those little snippets of extra personal time. In the end, though, if salaried workers quit their job, their income stops too. That means it is active income. Activity is required to keep the income going. The list of active income types is pretty short. Here it is:

- Job
- Business Owner (sometimes)

You are making active income anytime you work for somebody else for a paycheck. You must keep working to keep getting paid. Even some business owners are like this. Many small business owners might have more control over their work environment, but they still have a job. They still have to be there in order to make money. If you start your own small lawn mowing business, you have to mow the lawns to make money. Your activity is required to keep the income flowing.

> **HIGHLIGHT:** Many small business owners are still workers. If they stop working, their income stops.

Passive

Income that you get without having to work for it is passive income. Passive income is the type of income that controllers use to gain their personal time. While active income is the easiest to understand, passive income usually requires more thought, planning, and understanding. Just about anybody can walk into a fast-food restaurant and make an agreement to trade their time for some money in the form of a job. Little knowledge is required up front, and the risk of losing any money is very low.

Let's talk briefly now about four types of passive income:

- Royalties
- Rents
- Interest
- Business Income

Note that these sources of "free" money often require your time up front in order to gain money later.

Royalties are income that you receive from the sale or continued use of something that you own. U.S. patents can be a good way to make royalties. By creating something new, unique, and valuable—and by protecting it with a patent—you are then able to license your idea, which means that companies might incorporate your idea into their products or services with an agreement that you will get a portion of the profit for every sale they make. Writing songs is very similar. Write a song, record it, sign a publishing contract and you will get a portion of every sale in the form of a royalty check. The same thing happens with writing computer applications or smart phone apps. Each sale of a product containing your original creation nets you some income long after you completed the work.

Rents are a more easily understood type of passive income. Anytime you allow people to use something and they pay you money to do so, you are renting. You can rent cars, apartments, storage units, and so forth. In these cases, you own the items and agree to let others use them for a specified time period for a certain fee. Renting out advertising space on your website is another way to bring in income through renting. Subscription-type activities can also make rental income by allowing people access to information that you have on a time-limited basis.

Interest is the money you make when you in essence become the banker. In fact, interest is really just rent earned from using your money instead of your things. You can be the lender through (1) direct money loans to your friends (maybe ill-advised, maybe not), (2) buying bonds, and (3) by getting an interest-bearing savings account. In the case of savings accounts, you deposit money into a bank, which then loans your money to other people. You get a small percentage of what the bank earns back from the borrower as a fee for the bank using your money to make money for itself. This mode of passive income is not usually all that productive, but it is a fairly low-risk prospect for you.

Last in our list of types of passive income is business income (cash flow income). I call business income money that you make from an active business that you own. The key is that you make this passive income by owning the business, not by running the business. If you have to be there for it to work, it is not really passive income. Buying stocks is a great way to be a business owner without having to do anything. You own a very small portion of a company, and you might get dividend checks if the company does well. Dividend checks are some of the profits of the company split up among all of the owners (stockholders) and usually are distributed on a quarterly basis. The downside of stocks is that you usually own a very small amount and have no control over how the company operates. If you own the entire company, or a majority of it, you can dictate what the company does. With ownership, you also assume greater risk and greater potential for profit.

How Passive is Passive?

Not all income is clearly active or passive, though. Few things are truly 100% passive (hands-free) for any length of time. So it's better to think about the degree to which something is passive. In other words, is it a one-for-one activity or is the ratio better than that? Most jobs are close to 0% passive because you have to be there for a specific amount of time in order to get paid, and you only get paid for your actual time at the worksite. On the other end of the spectrum is a situation in which something is completely hands-free and remains so for a length of time—being passive for as long as possible is the ideal. Let's say you take a truly superb photograph, one that is incredibly good that everybody loves. If you can give that image to a company that will promote it, sell it, and send you royalty checks without your involvement—and this goes on for a long time, years or decades—that would be 100% passive income.

Completely passive income requires none of your time, so it is essentially a one-for-nothing ratio. Some jobs and most instances of business ownership fall into the gray zone between 0% and 100% passive. Let's go back to the example of running a lawn mowing business, which was briefly mentioned at the end of the section on active income. When it was just you and a lawn mower, and you earned $12 an hour, you were 0% passive and had no leverage. If you grow your company and hire five employees to help you out, your ratio improves. You probably still have to be there most of the time, but you are now at least using leverage. No longer are you a one-for-one worker. You are a something like a two-for-one worker. You gain benefit or income from the time spent by each of your new employees. The additional income you gain from each of your employees is the hourly sales rate for each employee ($20) minus what each one costs you in pay and benefits. Paying each one $10 an hour with an operating cost for each one of $8 gives you an income of $2 for each employee ($20 - $18 = $2). That $2 is the profit you make from the time spent by each employee. If you had worked alone, you would have earned only $12 an hour, what you were earning when you were a solo act. But now you are leveraging all five of your employees so that you are now earning $22 per hour ($12 + $10). Your business is not very passive, but you are using leverage to improve your position. Clearly, it is pretty difficult, and often not a good idea, to create things that are completely passive or hands-off.

There are two potential issues with highly passive businesses. First, if you are not actively involved, you begin to lose control over how things operate. As a founder of a company, it was likely your passion, innovation, commitment, and care for the customer that made the venture successful. If you hire a manager and step away, how sure are you that your values, ideas, passion, customer service, and ethics will stay the same? If they falter, your business might decline, and so will your income.

The second issue is competition. Highly passive businesses by definition are hands-off. You are involved in neither running the system nor improving it. If you create a system that provides income for you with the ability to be hands-off, you can be pretty sure that other people will want to do the same thing. They might challenge you with a better product, better marketing, better service, or lower price. The more successful you are, the more likely it is that your competition will increase. It's only natural. If you learned of something that provided income with little to no use of your time, wouldn't you try your hand at it?

> **MYTH:** *100% passive income is the best way to make money.* While highly passive income might work well for a short period, it often does not last for long.

By letting your system or enterprise run on autopilot, you are inviting inevitable obsolescence. Somebody will eat your lunch through competition, the technology will change, or consumer desires will change. Since change is inevitable in the world, your system must change over time as well. The best way to make sure that it changes in a productive manner is for you, the creator, to be involved. Some people find that moderate levels of passivity combined with both leverage and passion are a potent mix for succeeding in a competitive environment. But again, this all depends on what your definition of success is.

In summary, active income requires your time. Passive income does not require your time because there is a system in place that provides an income stream without your involvement. Many systems that you could create will be a mix of active and passive income through the use of leverage. Leverage is gained by using other people's time, money, or resources to increase the efficiency of your income-earning ability. Leverage improves your time ratio from one-for-one, which is purely active, to something better. Active income is readily available in most modern societies. Just about anybody can walk into a business and apply for a job or start some kind of business where they do all of the work. Passive income and leverage normally require an initial investment of time, creativity, and money, and they often carry a higher level of risk than does most active income. If you lose your job, there is little immediate risk beyond your own loss of income. The income flow just stops. If your leveraged system fails, not only does your income likely stop but you might lose your initial investment or owe money to those you were leveraging.

Systems

In previous sections we mentioned the concept of systems. People can create systems to provide income through businesses, investments, and the like. Controllers create, control, and gain benefit from systems. But how and why do systems work? Why is there such a disparity in the wealth of our population? Our society contains a mix of large and small systems, and everybody has a role to play in them. Recognizing how systems work, the impacts of systems on your daily life, your place in systems, and the fact that they are natural and normal parts of society will help you to see your path a little more clearly.

What Are Systems?

So what are systems, and why are they everywhere? Systems are a collection of things that work together to provide an outcome. They can also be thought of as processes or sets of operations that must be performed to reach an outcome. Systems are abundant in the natural world, and mankind has learned to create its own systems.

A system usually contains an imbalance. There is more of one thing in it than of another thing. This imbalance is the force that drives the system and makes it operate so that an outcome occurs. This is a very important idea in society that we will revisit later, but first let's look at natural systems containing imbalances.

The weather is a prime example of a system that works due to imbalances. The sun causes temperature and humidity changes that can cause pressure changes in the atmosphere. When two levels of a particular thing develop in a natural system, the system tries to level things out again. In order to do this leveling, things begin to move. Hot air rises up to find an equal pressure. The change in temperature between the tropics and the arctic areas creates the jet stream. Wind blows from high pressure toward low pressure. All of this movement and action is caused by a difference in something.

The natural world runs on disparity. Systems in the natural world require some kind of difference, or imbalance, to function. The only energy ever added to the system on this planet is sunlight. The rest of the system runs solely on differences in energy. Night and day. Dark and light. High pressure and low pressure. Hot and cold. Grass grows, gazelles graze, lions kill, carcasses rot, and the grass grows once more.

> **HIGHLIGHT:** Systems function because of differences or disparity.

This simple cycle appears frequently in nature. Human beings use the same principles nature does. We create systems to provide outcomes, just like nature does. Let's look at a car, for example. Once the car has been designed and built, you simply add fuel and it operates. The engine converts the stored energy of sunshine in oil to horsepower and heat with a little nudge of energy known as the spark plug. The differences in pressure and heat make the system work. Once the car is built, the owner just has to guide it along in the right direction and enjoy the benefits.

These laws of disparity, of differences driving systems to function, also apply to people. A business is a system that can be thought of as an engine. Somebody creates the system and then operates it while enjoying the benefits. Instead of producing horsepower and heat like a car engine, a business creates value or wealth. Instead of using pistons and gears, a business must generally use machines and people as tools in the system. The deeper questions are why some people start businesses, why most people work in them, and why there is generally tension between those who create systems and those who work in them.

Why does a river flow toward the sea? It flows because of a difference in height between where it starts and where the sea is. The water is trying to find the lowest possible level due to gravity. If you took physics in school, you probably learned about kinetic and potential energy. These two types of energy exist in nature as the drivers of systems.

Interestingly, something very similar happens in society. There are differences between all of us that help to not only drive systems to function but to create the systems as well. We all have different levels of desire, creativity, motivation, and intelligence, for example. These differences allow our society to grow and flourish. Idlers have very low energy. Workers create more kinetic energy than idlers through greater activity and have a higher potential to make money although they might not use that potential. Controllers build up a high potential energy first and then turn it into kinetic energy. Creating a system or a business is creating potential energy. Writing a song is creating potential energy. As soon as the business opens or the song goes up for sale, that potential is turned into kinetic energy or profit.

Money, like water, flows from person to person due to disparity. You have money that I don't, and I have something of value that you don't. We trade money for items to try to balance out our own personal value equation. If I have 100 copies of a book, one of those copies has less value to me than it might to you because you don't have any at all. You might happily trade some money, which I value more than an extra copy of the book, for a book that you don't have. Society functions by these "have" and "have not" disparities. Satisfying the needs and desires people have for things often requires their interaction with others.

Society has changed greatly in the 250+ years since the beginning of the Industrial Revolution. During that transition period in Europe and America, people began to create systems that very efficiently created disparity. Instead of building a car in his garage over the course of two years, Henry Ford created a system to create many cars in a much shorter timeframe. Did Henry Ford need that many cars for himself? Of course not. What he did was create a great disparity between himself and all those who both wanted cars and had enough money to buy them. He had a lot of cars and was willing to sell them to those who wanted them, and then the money began to flow.

In the early days of human society, most activity happened at the individual level. There weren't corporations, employers, or great systems. People often did what they needed to do to survive. If they needed food, they hunted. If they needed shelter from the weather, they built a place of protection from the elements by hand. If they needed weapons or tools, they made them by hand as well. Each person had little leverage and no ability to use systems. As time passed and people's skills improved, they were able to create more of certain things than they needed themselves. These extra items could be traded for items that they needed or wanted but didn't have. This system of trade eventually allowed people to focus on a specific skill and produce much more of one thing than anything else. Such behavior gave rise to farmers, blacksmiths, bakers, basket makers, and other tradespeople. These people did what they knew how to do efficiently and traded for the things that they did not have time or knowledge to do quite as well. As we discussed earlier, various forms of money helped to ease these transactions. Back then, pretty much everyone was an idler or a worker, except the king or ruler.

The growth of specialized or focused activities led to the early forms of business systems. Slavery, indentured servitude, and employees of newly formed businesses were used as leverage to create wealth. The invention of true companies, the appearance of machines of increasing complexity, and eventually the beginning of the Industrial Revolution further developed the concept of leverage. People who were the original controllers were actively planning and creating systems that could provide large amounts of income through leverage. Larger businesses began to provide passive income by hiring managers to run the companies in the absence of the owners. The number of people moving from subsistence or self-employment to the ranks of the employed dramatically increased.

Similar to the Industrial Revolution's effect on creating things that could be sold, the computer revolution of the past 40 years has done the same with communication and information. Businesses and people have much greater access to information, and transactions with people they wouldn't normally have access to have become much easier. Before the Internet was available, you likely would have either sold your goods or services only locally or had to use some kind of marketing and distribution network outside of your control. If you created a kitchen tool, for example, you would have to produce it and then try to sell it through your own store or to a larger network of brick-and-mortar stores. If the distributor or the stores didn't like your item or didn't want to sell it for some reason, you were out of luck. Now you can easily create a website to sell your item directly to the public or you can sell it through some other online network where ordering, warehousing, and distribution are simpler than a brick-and-mortar store's processes and where the online system can accommodate a far greater number of items for sale than can any one brick-and-mortar store. As mentioned earlier, anything that makes it easier to create money and is at all passive will attract more competition.

That is why computer science and the Internet are full of people trying to make money. The Internet is a gigantic system or tool that many people are using to create active and passive income with greater ease than ever before. The Internet also can slow the rate at which people become employees of companies. All types of people use the Internet, and it is fairly easy for anyone with a computer to create a website and start selling goods and services. You no longer need large industrial marketing and distribution companies if you want to sell goods and services around the world. Just about anyone can hang out their dot com sign and be in business for themselves.

Your Place

Commercial systems operate with two sides called the producer side and the consumer side. Seems pretty obvious right? One group or side of the system is producing things (the business) that get consumed by the other side (the buying public), which doesn't have them. In other words, there is a disparity. A system can be used to produce many things, including cars, information, or entertainment. Idlers, workers, and controllers are all necessary to make systems work. You'll need to select and understand your place in the systems as either the producer (controller) or consumer (worker or idler). Without consumers there would be no need for producers. Without lots of consumers willing to spend money, there would be little incentive to create new systems or businesses to produce the items in the first place. Systems and businesses need demand (people willing to buy the products and services offered by businesses) in order to succeed. They need to solve a problem or fill a need for enough people so they can at least break even. If they cannot do that, they are not viable businesses and will quickly cease to operate.

Idlers are consumers, but are typically low-level consumers because they lack disposable income, which is money left over after you pay your basic expenses such as food and shelter. Idlers might spend much of their disposable money, or use credit, on entertainment. Entertainment or enjoyment is one of those short-term success goals that most of us share. Idlers will often focus on that short-term, feel-good success in the form of watching TV or movies, playing games, or surfing the Internet. These activities are all entertainment. Individuals have produced these forms of entertainment in an effort to make money from consumers, and many of these people have become very good at it. Even if you don't pay anything to read a website, there will almost certainly be advertisements for goods on that site. When people buy the items advertised, they are providing money to pay for the website. Very little in the world is actually free. If you didn't pay, it is very likely that somebody else did.

Workers are also consumers. They work in a system and therefore in theory produce something, but they probably didn't create or invent the item and they rarely benefit from the production of it other than through a paycheck. It is common for workers to focus on consumption early in their working lives and to do so more aggressively than they focus on investing or controlling activities. Workers are employed within a system and use their pay to go out and consume. In the United States, the middle class, which is mostly workers, is an overly active group of consumers. With all of that desire to spend money, there is a never-ending supply of systems designed to produce and sell items in exchange for profits, the money spent by workers. For decades, the mantra of the middle class has been to get a good education, get a good job, buy some of the things that you want, and save a little for a rainy day and eventually retirement. This is the path of the average consumer. Work hard, save a little, reward yourself, and repeat.

There is nothing inherently wrong with choosing to be a worker as your place in the system. Millions of people follow this path and lead fairly happy and successful lives. Remember that success is totally defined by you and what you feel is important. Many people like the seemingly predictable nature of working for others. Perhaps they enjoy their area of expertise and don't want to deal with the other aspects of creating or running a system. The systems, in return, need these people. The only real drawback is that since so many people follow this path, it is difficult to amass much wealth from it. In addition, following this path takes a lot of your time. It is especially difficult to amass wealth quickly as a worker. If, however, you desire something different from your life's journey, perhaps more wealth or more personal time, then perhaps your place in the system is on the producer side. You need to be a controller who creates and benefits from these systems. You need to focus on being a producer first and a consumer second. Success in terms of wealth usually requires leverage (a system) or scarcity (a rare singing talent, for example), or both. If you don't have a physical or artistic talent that is in high demand and low supply, you would be better off starting a system if you want to put the odds in your favor.

HIGHLIGHT: The worker might enjoy a comfortable level of income, but becoming wealthy is difficult due to the vast number of people with whom they compete.

The Power of Systems

Systems can be incredibly powerful. Think of the system that was required to put a man on the moon. All of those minds, the organization, the vision, and the ultimate physical machines created were all leveraged to accomplish a single outcome. Much of the vision and guidance of that vast system came from a handful of people who used that enormous leverage to achieve their dream. What could you achieve if you had that amount of leverage at your disposal?

The ever-increasing pace of system creation and the growing complexity of systems are having a dramatic impact on the way people live. These systems, at least in many modern societies, have made it possible to achieve a comfortable life with relatively little effort. Basic goods and services are produced very efficiently and are affordable to just about everyone. One of the drawbacks to this situation is the ease with which one can become an idler and maintain the idler lifestyle. If your focus is very near-term, and your definition of success fits that lifestyle, there is little stopping you from living as an idler. Buying a bag of beef jerky is much cheaper and easier to do than hunting down and killing your snack, as you would have had to do centuries ago.

The power of systems can be used to your benefit no matter which path you choose—idler, worker, or controller. Just make sure you understand which side of the system you are on compared to where you want to go. Compare your version of success with the average outcome of each group and let that help you determine your actions and path forward.

Size of Each Category

Idlers, workers, and controllers all play a role in our society. The systems require each of these categories in order to operate. Controllers create the systems. Workers, and sometimes idlers, labor in the systems. Both idlers and workers consume what the systems produce. Controllers consume as well, but there are usually fewer of them than there are idlers and workers. A pertinent question here is how many people are in each category. It is estimated that 5.4 million people graduated from high school, two-year or four-year college programs in 2009 in the US.[1,2] The total workforce for those between 20 and 24 was just over 15 million in 2010.[3] That is a lot of people entering into an already massive system. Where do you want to be in relation to all of those people?

It is difficult to find statistics about successful people due to the fact that the definition of success varies from person to person. We can, however, use net worth or income to differentiate idlers, workers, and controllers. Although we will have to assume some things about each group that won't be 100% true, we can still get a decent idea of group membership. Let's take 2012 as an example, and assume that idlers made less than $25K that year and had virtually no net worth, which means that they had no savings or investments and that they didn't own anything of significant value, such as a home. Let's then assume that workers, being the largest group, made between $25K and $250K of income in 2012. Their net worth ranged from nothing to somewhere around $1 million. Let's finally assume that controllers made more than $250K in 2012 and/or had a net worth above $1 million. Some controllers who were just getting started in creating their systems in 2012 might not be in this group, but that's because they were still workers who were in the midst of creating and setting up their systems.

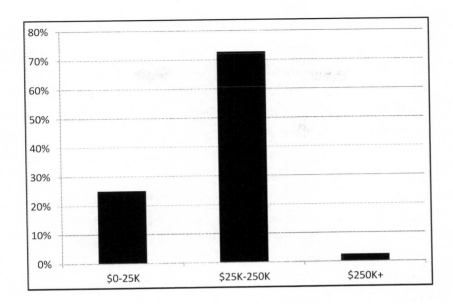

Figure 5.1: Percent of U.S. Households vs.
Income Bracket [4]

As you can see from Figure 5.1, the idlers and workers outnumber the controllers by at least 42 to 1. It should also be clear that it is easier to become a worker than it is to become a controller. Most controllers got to where they are not by luck alone, but by smart choices, hard work, and just a little luck. The fact that it takes effort, conscious choices, vision, and education (formal or informal) keeps most people away from the path of the controller. By education, I don't necessarily mean classroom education in the usual sense. The education I'm referring to is the acquisition of knowledge about and an awareness of the fact that systems can be created and used to increase business effectiveness. Learning about how such systems work can help one to pursue the path of a controller. Such information is easy to obtain today. People can be fortunate enough that somebody tells them about systems, or they can search for the information on their own. How often have you searched the Internet for music videos? How often have you searched for options or guidance on your path through life? Your habits, your choices, your attitudes, and your definition of success will walk you down one of these paths whether you are paying attention or not.

What This Means to You

Being a part of a system is an unavoidable aspect of living in this world. We are surrounded by them and involved in them all the time. Whether they are natural systems that create rain or man-made systems that produce and sell you shoes, systems are unavoidable. Systems need disparity or inequality in order to operate. Our society, especially the monetary side, functions because there are differences between people. Disparity is normally the cause of systems and not the symptom or result. Some people have things or choose to do things that others do not, be that motivation, natural talents, or having lots of something that other people want. Money will naturally flow between people based on what they each value and tends to end up where it is most valued. Idlers value time, so money doesn't tend to head their way. Workers commonly value things, so they trade money and time for them. Controllers value time and money more than things, so that is what they focus on first. Some of the keys to figuring out your path through life are to recognize these systems, understand how they operate, and consciously decided where you want to be in them.

Your position in the systems, combined with what you focus on, will be important in your life's path. If you continually focus on consuming, it will be very hard to become a producer or controller and you will probably follow either the idler or worker path. Focusing on investing and creating systems will likely lead you down the controller path.

THINK WHERE YOU'RE GOING

Part 2

People

THINK WHERE YOU'RE GOING

6

You and Your Values

I learned this, at least, by my experiment; that if one
advances confidently in the direction of his dreams, and
endeavors to live the life which he has imagined, he will
meet with success unexpected in common hours.
-Henry David Thoreau

Understanding People

As you begin this next chapter in your life, you will meet and interact with a wide variety of people. Some of these people will be ones that you have known for a long time as family and friends. Some will be new in your life, such as new friends, bosses, coworkers, and perhaps a spouse or significant other. Another new person in your life might actually be you. This is probably a time of personal growth and change that will make you a different person than you were a few years ago or even than who you are today. Having a basic understanding of people, including yourself, will help you to navigate through your chosen path with greater ease.

Values

Let's talk about you a bit more. To pick a path that you wish to travel requires that you examine your values. What is important to you in the near term and in the long run? What principles do you expect will guide you on your journey through life? In school you might have struggled to stay true to your values due to peer pressure or just the natural changes taking place inside you. Now, at graduation, is a fantastic time to look directly at your values and make plans to change anything you might want to do differently from now on.

After you leave school, maybe you will live at home with your parents. Maybe, on the other hand, within a few short weeks or months you will be living in a new place in which you are exposed to new people. These people won't know your past or really know who you are. If you are happy with the person you have become, that's great. Keep sticking to your values and principles and carry on. If you find that the person in the mirror isn't really who you want to be, take this chance to make some changes. These times of transition in life, times when we are forced out of the ruts of our everyday lives, are good opportunities to change. Making some changes to yourself might be easier and less noticeable to others if things are already in some level of turmoil. You can literally walk into your new job with the mind-set that you are a new person. If you believe that you are a new person and act accordingly, you *are* a new person. Those people you meet now will only know the person you show them.

Your values are the things that are important to you. These things are deep within you, and only you really know what they are. Values are not physical things. They are feelings or actions or results in general that you find to be important. You might value friendships, close family ties, charity, or honesty. If you find that a certain high-end car brand is important to you, you probably value those things that the car stands for, not really the car itself. Those things might be quality, performance, or high social status.

What you value and the order, or priority, in which you value them play a big part in setting you on your path through life. You will find that much of your happiness and your personal success will depend on your values and how true you are to them. An internal conflict or unhappiness might be a result of your actions not matching up with your values. Do you deeply value your personal time but agree to volunteer for extra hours at work? That would be a conflict and probably cause you some uneasiness. Valuing honesty will again cause you problems if you tell a lie or do something dishonest. It is pretty tough to fool your inner self.

Quiz Review

Look back at your Total Score from the "What Do You Want Out of Life?" quiz in chapter 1. Locate that score on the scale in Figure 6.1, which will show you where you roughly lie on the continuum from idler to controller. Remember, there is no right or wrong place to be. The only thing that matters is that your vision of success matches up with your values and thought patterns. If they don't match up very well right now, you have a chance to make some changes. If you have a high score, you can choose a spot anywhere on the chart and be any of the three types. If you scored lower, it will be harder for you to move around on the chart unless you take some deliberate action.

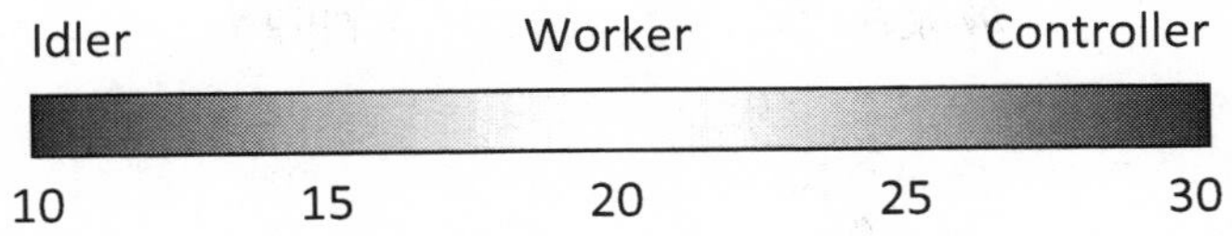

Idler		Worker		Controller
10	15	20	25	30

Figure 6.1: Quiz Scoring Review

Evaluate what you value now versus what you will likely, or wish to, value later. Decide which path or category will suit you best and allow you to become successful based on your values. If you've been following along, I can bet that you can probably list some values of each category of person and how they are ranked. Let's start with the idler. Idlers might value their personal time, having fun, friendships, freedom, and spontaneity. They might value a great many things, including family, their health, happiness, or compassion. Depending on their personality, they might highly value their privacy. The funny thing is that most people, whether they are idlers, workers, or controllers, will list nearly the same values. Unless you are a sociopath, you probably have about the same values as everyone else. The difference between the categories is which values have a higher importance than the others.

You might have heard the expression "You only do what you want to do." That is a very profound concept when you take time to think about it and how it relates to your values. Unless someone has a gun to your head, and even then, you will make the choice that reflects your values. If somebody actually puts a gun to your head and tells you to rob a bank or else, what would you do? Assuming you value both your life and being an honest, law-abiding person, you are faced with a decision that will be based on which you value more. I, for one, would rob the bank, as I value my life more than I value following the law in this case. Here is a less extreme example. Losing weight is a common goal. Imagine that you are trying to lose weight because you value your health and outward appearance. Monday morning finds you at your new job, and a coworker brings in a box of fresh, hot donuts that smell fantastic. They are even your favorite kind. As you stand there and stare at the box, you probably feel a conflict. You want to eat one, but you also want to stick to your diet. What you feel is your brain trying to figure out in that moment which values—enjoyment and self-satisfaction or health and outward appearance—are highest on your list. If you eat the donut, you are saying that health and outward appearance, while important values, are not the most important ones. At least they aren't right at that moment. You ate the donut because you wanted to enjoy it more than you wanted to lose weight.

The same thing applies to how you value time and money. These two things are what separate the idlers, workers, and controllers. I use "money" here as a catchall for the values money helps one attain. These values might be freedom, spontaneity, security, and the ability to provide these things for your family; luxury; quality items; charity; or helping others. Money itself isn't what you value; it is what money stands for or what it can provide for you that you value. People in each category will value time and money, but they will not consistently rank either value the same. Idlers will value short-term things like having fun, freedom, and perhaps friendships more than they will value long-term security and wealth. They might actually value all of these things, but their actions will show which is really most important to them, and it often isn't a close call. True idlers will go for their immediate success, with little thought about values that relate to the future. If they are hungry, they might eat potato chips and fast-food, because the value of health is much lower than enjoyment or convenience.

Workers probably have the most conflict when it comes to values. Since these people have one eye on the now and one eye on the future, their value system is constantly tested. Many of the common values that we all share end up closely ranked in the level or order of importance. Family, personal time, long-term security, enjoyment, and appearing to be wealthy or happy or successful are all values that they might hold that compete to be number one. Starting a savings account and then going out and buying a new car might cause a worker some internal conflict or feelings of guilt. They value long-term security and perhaps their personal time, to some degree, which is why they started a savings account. Having feelings of guilt or remorse about buying a new car might indicate that the values that the car stands for, the appearance of success, quality, performance, and so on, are in conflict with those that prompted starting a savings account. Knowing that a brand-new car is not really necessary, and that most of that money could have gone into the savings account, will result in stress, guilt, anxiety, or remorse when the value of long-term security bubbles back up to the top of their list of values. These oscillations or changes in values happen over a relatively short time span, such as hours or days. There might be many causes for these shifting values, but a primary cause is likely that many people do not have a clear understanding of the ramifications of their actions.

Controllers share many of the same values as idlers and workers, but several values hold a much higher or stronger ranking in their mind. When faced with a decision, they will often make the choice that is more beneficial to long-term values and bypass short-term values. Some of this behavior might be caused by controllers having either an instinct or a better understanding of how decisions made now will affect their future. They might have thought through their lives with a little more effort and created a plan, however rough, to get to where they want to be. This plan or vision of the future is very important to them and causes their values of freedom, financial independence, security, and other long-range values to be highest in their internal value system.

Controllers value personal time and enjoyment right now, but they know that indulging in those things today might jeopardize the things that they value the most. Because they have thought more about these topics and their desired path through life, their values are spaced more widely apart from each other according to their priority or strength. Contrast that with the worker whose values are all very closely ranked and can alternate in order of importance quite easily.

Figure 6.2 shows an example set of values for an idler in a vertical list, with the more important values at the top and the less important at the bottom. The values at the top of the list will be the ones that idlers seek to satisfy most often.

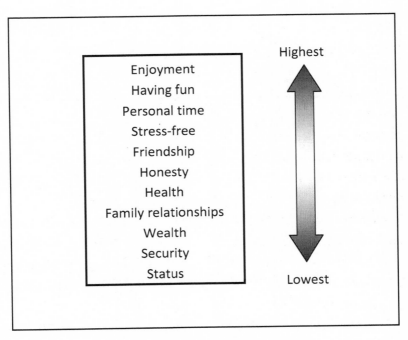

Figure 6.2: Idler Value System Example

Figure 6.3 shows the same list of values but has them arranged without any particular order. For the worker, these values will shift frequently and will not have a clear, consistent ranking.

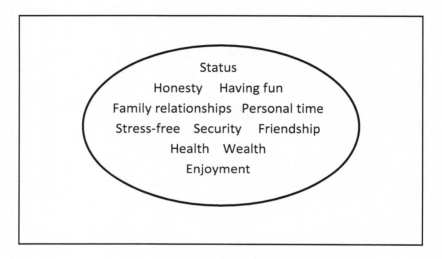

Figure 6.3: Worker Value System Example

Figure 6.4 is for controllers. Again, the same values appear for controllers as appear for idlers and workers. The values are arranged in a vertical list similar to the list for idlers. The values that are concerned with longer-term successes and, importantly, long-term security and freedom are higher on their list than on the idlers' list. Controllers still value fun and their personal time, but those values are lower than the future or long-term values.

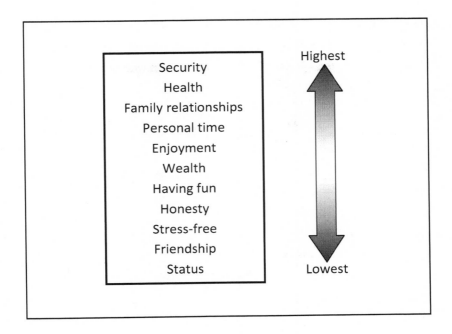

Figure 6.4: Controller Value System Example

Values change over time because we as people change over time. Having your values change over longer periods of time is normally a good and natural thing. As we mature, gain experience, and have our life situations shift, our value levels might gradually shift as well. Perhaps you didn't grow up in a close-knit family, and so the value of family ties and relationships is not as strong for you as for others. Over the years, your attitude can shift, either through new life experiences or because you start a family of your own and discover the value of family relationships for the first time. Falling in love and having children will almost certainly shift your values around. Your attitudes and values relating to family relationships probably won't shift quickly. It might take months or years to change your value system for things that really matter.

Shifts in the ranking of your values that happen quickly are where conflict comes into play and can cause you trouble. If you experience rapidly changing desires and make choices that don't seem to have a pattern or common theme, you are likely experiencing a flat value system. What this means is that your value system doesn't have higher-ranked values that are clearly discerned and lower-ranked values that are equally clearly discerned. You might need to take some time to reflect on your values and your long-term goals and definition of success in an effort to strengthen a few of those values that can guide you on a straighter path. What do you value, what is important to you, are you proud that you value what you value? What would happen if you didn't value those things as much as something else? Where are your values likely to take you in life? You probably know the answers to these questions. Just be honest with yourself, and if you don't like the answers, you can start to work on changing things. The first step is knowing.

A word of caution is due here, however. Just because a certain value is at the top of your list doesn't mean you should ignore the rest of them. Life requires a certain balance to be whole. Pursuing health, wealth, or fun at the expense of everything else might leave you in just as much trouble or more than pursuing none of them at all.

An Exercise

Take a few moments and write down some of your most important values. Make it your Top 10 or so and try to list them in order of importance if you can. Do this with sincerity and honesty, trying to list the things that are really important to you. After you're finished, think back over the last week, and compare your actions to your value list. Did they match up pretty well, somewhat, or not at all? Do you think that the things that you did and the choices you made are leading toward success according to your values? It is easy to lose sight of our value list in the day-to-day world. I encourage you to think about your values frequently in order to keep yourself on track to achieving your goals. Perhaps you can repeat this exercise on your birthday, New Year's, or maybe the first of every month.

Vision

Having a vision for your future is crucial if you want to be able to chart a path for your life that you are in control of. Values and vision are closely related. The vision of your life will be the expected manifestation or achievement of your values. If the vision of your future has you working in Africa for an aid organization, you likely value compassion, honesty, and action fairly highly. A vision of a large house and luxury cars might be the expected result of valuing wealth and status. A cozy home filled with family and friends has its own set of driving values. Whatever it is that you envision, you probably won't achieve it unless your values align with it.

You certainly can head out into the world without a vision. A lot of people do. Many of those people end up in the idler category, and many end up as workers. Virtually nobody ends up as a controller without a vision. As we mentioned in the previous section on values, workers can have a difficult time identifying a set of values with clear ranking because they might have a weak vision or no vision at all. Having no vision is like driving a car without a map or even having a destination in mind that would require a map. You can drive, sure, but you will just wander around, heading down any street that seems like the right one at the time. Having a weak vision is like knowing that you want to get to a big city, but not knowing which one. You might have a map, but you don't really look at it that much. Workers often have a vision of wealth and security, but there isn't much detail (there is no name on the city they are heading for), and they don't revisit their vision and values very often (they don't look at the map). Controllers try to have a pretty clear vision, with perhaps some near-term goals or milestones, and they revisit their vision, values, challenges, and successes frequently. They know where they are heading, they have a map, and they use it.

Having a vision and a set of values that align with it will help you to stay on course and to navigate life's inevitable rough spots. If you played volleyball or other sports in school, you might have already experienced the truth of this. You and your team had shared values and a shared vision. You probably valued hard work, fair play, and success. The team's vision could have been beating a long-standing rival, winning its first game ever, or winning a championship. You might have had more personal visions of getting a personal best or being noticed by a college scout. In order to achieve those visions, you had to act according to your values. Long, grueling practices, studying yourselves and your opponents on video, and doing school homework late at night after practices are all part of the hard-work value. That hard work might have been a little easier when you thought about your vision and what it would feel like to attain it. If you had no vision of a future success, would you have stuck to it when practice was hard, painful, and frustrating? Certainly not every game or competition would have gone as planned, leading to feelings of doubt or frustration as well. Did you give up at the first sign of a challenge? Did the team disband after you lost three games in a row? No. Why not? Because you had a vision of success in the future that you were striving for, and you knew that setbacks weren't the end of the road—they were only a part of it. The setbacks weren't fun, but you knew that achieving success would be well worth it. Life is just like that. You set your vision, watch your values, and head on down the road. Challenges will arise, problems will occur, and you will get sidetracked from time to time. That is all completely natural and expected. Those with a clear vision and values to match can make it through those obstacles easier. Lacking a clear vision or a value set that you understand might lead you to get sidetracked longer, or even permanently, when you hit one of life's little bumps because there will be nothing for you to focus on other than the immediate problem. Deal with problems, but don't get lost in them. How do you not get lost? Use your map of values and vision.

Long vs. Short

Life is a long road, or at least we all hope that it is. Setting a goal or vision for your life right now might seem like an impossible thing. Even if you think that you know what your vision is, how long do you expect it will take to achieve it? Are you thinking of a comfortable retirement at 65? That might just well be over 45 years away, which is a long time. Spending 45 years working toward a single vision sounds daunting, and I would think that the chances of getting lost somewhere along the way are pretty high. Breaking up your path into smaller pieces is one way to help you stick to your path.

Let's say you want to drive from your college in Chicago to Miami right after graduation for a short vacation. You can almost feel the hot sun, warm water, sea breeze, and white sand. Awesome idea, right? You have a vision, and success to you is reaching Miami in two days. A hotel room is booked starting at the end of the second day, and you and two friends jump in the car and hit the road. Step one of achieving any vision is starting toward it. From there you have two options for making the trip. Option one is to just go with the flow and head south. You have a map or smart phone, but no real plan other than the desire to be at the beach in two days. The other option is to think through the trip and put a little plan together. It wouldn't have to be an elaborate plan, but just enough to break the trip up into manageable pieces. It is 1,400 miles, after all.

Option one would likely start out just fine. You all head out of the windy city on familiar roads, full of excitement. About three hours later, you find yourself in Indianapolis, and you stop for lunch. One of you has heard of a cool restaurant, so you all decide to go there. It's a little out of the way, but hey, who's in a hurry? After lunch you start off again, get back on track and head south. Dinnertime finds you nearing Nashville. Come on, it's Nashville. Where better to have dinner and hear some music? Good food, fun people, and a hot band make it hard to leave. A few of your favorite songs, a few dances, and before you know it, it's getting close to midnight. Nobody wants to drive much further, so you decide to spend the night in Nashville. A cheap hotel room is located down the street from the venue you're at, and so you continue the fun until the wee hours.

The next morning starts late, naturally, and you barely make checkout at 11:00 a.m. Famished, you find a pancake shop and have a leisurely late breakfast. Refreshed, you pile back into the car and finally head out. A missed exit causes a 30-minute delay, but by 2:00 p.m. you are finally on your way again. The goal you set is Atlanta, since one of you has an old friend who lives there. About four hours later you roll into Atlanta and are hungry again. The old friend meets up for dinner with you and your two friends, and everyone has a great time. He insists that you all crash at his place, since it is now close to 10:00 p.m. and you aren't quite fully recovered from the night before. It's an easy choice and a night is spent in Atlanta, but you skip the party scene this time.

You know you are behind schedule, so you get up early, ok maybe at 9:00 a.m., and get going. You are now about nine hours from Miami, which should easily be doable today. The morning flies by and the afternoon goes pretty fast as well. Lunch is on the road, but by Orlando your legs need some stretching. A little detour finds you at a great restaurant that serves margaritas and has an airplane parked outside surrounded by palm trees. The sun feels so good that you linger a while as it sets. You know that it's still over three hours to Miami, so you drag yourselves back to the car and speed off. The rush of Miami is around you by 10:30 p.m., and it takes you another hour or so to locate the hotel you booked. Wait, what day is this, again? Let's see, you left on day one and spent that night in Nashville. Day two ended in Atlanta, and now it is late on day three. Your reservation was for yesterday and since you failed to show up or notify them within 24 hours, they gave your room to someone else according to their policy, which of course you didn't read. Now you are in Miami, a day late, with no place to stay and trying to find a hotel room at midnight.

The second option for the trip would have been to plan out the trip using smaller sections. You all decide ahead of time that in order to make it to Miami on the day that you want to, you have to make it to Atlanta on day one. It is a 10-hour drive to Atlanta, so lunch has to be on the road outside of Louisville, and you have to eat and get back on the road pretty quickly. Day two also is a long day, without time to stop much. If you hit Gainesville, FL, by lunch you should land at your hotel in Miami just after dinnertime.

What is the difference between the two scenarios? Both have the same long-term vision, which is to end up in Miami by the second night. The second one gets you there when you want to be there because you use shorter milestones to keep you on track and to judge your progress. If you realize that you are two hours late reaching your first milestone, you can adjust your plan. Without making any adjustments, the rate at which you are losing time could continue which would result in you being 12 hours late by the time you reach your destination. As the trip unfolds, you can adjust your travel plans, stop less, and drive more or call ahead and change your reservation. This simple example shows how breaking up your long-term plan or vision into smaller parts will help keep you moving toward your final goal with a better chance of success. It will also give you the option to make adjustments along the way as needed to avoid a potentially nasty surprise at the end.

Having a vision of being a millionaire, starting a charity organization, or becoming an engineer are all commendable goals. At the start of your journey toward one of these visions, achieving your goal might seem a lifetime away and nearly impossible. A very helpful strategy is to break the journey down into more manageable goals, just like in the driving example above.

Say you want to be an engineer. What are the steps needed to get there? Some of the steps may be to have earned good grades in high school and focused on science and math electives if they were offered. Maybe you joined the physics club. Next might be reading about and talking to engineers to get a feel for what each type of engineer does. Once you narrow done what type of engineer that you want to be, you can find some colleges that focus on that type of engineering discipline. Good grades are important during your college career, but so is getting real world experience. Ok, that means you need to find an internship, participate in a robotics competition or other opportunity. Looking towards graduation will bring about some possibilities to network or research firms that are either actively hiring or announcing the start of new projects. Crafting a resume and practicing how to interview are great steps toward landing that first job.

So you see, little by little you can work towards the end vision, but each little goal is much less intimidating and more easily achieved. When strung together, all of these little successes lead you toward your vision.

THINK WHERE YOU'RE GOING

7

Attitude

What a man thinks of himself, that it is which
determines, or rather indicates, his fate.
-Henry David Thoreau

Expectations and Accountability

Achieving your goals and visions, no matter what they are, will take effort on your part. You are the only person who is responsible for your life. The path of your life will, for the most part, be determined by the choices and actions that you take. If you take control and actively try to plan your life and take action, you have a much greater likelihood of being successful, no matter what being successful means to you. Leaving your life up to other people will not lead you down the path you desire.

Most people have expectations about almost everything. You expect the sun to come up every day. You expect that you will have gray hair when you are old. When somebody says that he or she will pick you up at a certain time, you expect that person to arrive at the given time. Expectations are a good thing. Having expectations means that you probably have some kind of a plan and have thought through some of the possible outcomes of whatever scenario you are facing. The problem with some expectations is that you rely very heavily on them, but often don't have much control over the actual outcome.

For example, getting great grades in high school and scoring well on the standard college entrance tests might make you overly confident about being accepted at your preferred college. If you only apply to your top choice college with the expectation that they will for sure select you, then you might end up in a tough situation. Their selection process is out of your hands and it might not go in your favor despite your expectations. Leaving the outcome up to somebody else without a backup plan of other schools would be foolish on your part. This is similar to the expectation that stock prices will always go up or that you will never get laid off from your job, so you don't need to save. Expectations can be a good thing, but be careful about the uncertainty of outcomes and who, if anyone, is in control of them.

I've been talking so far about your expectations of how you want things to be in the future. You have to be careful about how you think things *should* be in the future or even how they should be right now. The world is made up of all kinds of people and they live in all kinds of situations. You are a unique person living a unique life that is unlike anybody else's. It is common in our society for life to be portrayed in a stereotypical fashion through entertainment and other media sources. While this stereotype might be true for some, it most certainly isn't true for everyone, nor does it have to be. Even your family, friends, coworkers, or people at your church might present an image to the world that they think everyone else expects to see. That image, however, might not be completely reflective of what their day-to-day reality is.

Getting a job, finding a spouse, and moving to the suburbs could find you surrounded by people living in nice houses, buying new electronic gadgets, and driving nice cars. If you see and experience this image enough, you might come to believe that everybody is doing just fine, making money, getting rich, and living the dream. Closer examination, however, might reveal that all is not as it seems. According to the U.S. Census,[5,6] in 2011 the median household debt was $70,000, while the median net worth was only $68,828. Roughly one in five American households has a negative net worth.[6] The divorce rate is over 40%.[7] Thousands of children are born out of wedlock. There are many statistics similar to these, but they are not meant to depress you. They are just meant to show you that if you think everybody else is doing great or living a "perfect" life and that you are expected to be just like that, you might be chasing a ghost. Over 15 million new cars and trucks were sold in the United States in 2013.[8] That is a brand new car for 1 out of every 14 people between 18 and 65 years of age. Do you really think that one out of 14 people can really afford a brand new car each year in view of the statistics on debt just given? You need to figure out what success means to you and make a plan that works for you. Trying to meet somebody else's vision of success is going to be a tough road that not only won't be very smooth, but that also won't lead you to where you really want to go.

"Entitlement" might be a word that you are already familiar with. In reality, there is very little in life that you are entitled to or deserve to get, other than the freedom to live within our laws. You will be accountable for your own choices, your actions, and your position in life. It is primarily up to you to change things if you don't like your life.

Attitude and Emotional Intelligence (EI)

Now that you have looked at your values and your vision, how do you want to act as you go through your journey? How do you want to be seen by others? What impact do your thoughts and attitudes have on your ability to reach your goals? Your attitude and reactions to things around you and to the things that happen to you can have a dramatic impact on your ability to reach your goals.

Your attitude, both your attitude at any one moment and your attitude over longer periods, can have a big impact. Your attitude might affect your performance ability, energy level, and your decision making. Negative or defeatist attitudes will slow you down, lead you to make decisions that do not produce desirable outcomes, and usually put you in a sour mood overall. A negative attitude, even about just one aspect of your life, can also bleed over into other areas of your life and affect them. Many people find it difficult to fully compartmentalize their lives and their emotions. By "compartmentalize," I mean having the ability to not let work, relationships, or money matters affect the other aspects of our life. If you have a bad day at work or school, do you have the ability to switch off that part of your thoughts as soon as you walk out the door or do you find that any negativity follows you and affects other areas of your life? Can a rough day in one aspect cause you to jeopardize the other aspects? How many people do you know who get home after a tough day and then make a decision that isn't in line with the values that they would normally want to hold to? Getting home on Monday with a bad or downcast attitude, grabbing a bag of potato chips, and sitting on the couch might be contrary to the goals and values that you had when you thought about your life on Saturday.

Now I'm not saying that you should be bright and chipper with a great positive attitude all of the time. That is a pretty tough thing to do. Life has its ups and downs, but the trick is to know that it does and to pay attention to your reactions. Emotional Intelligence (EI) is a term that is used to describe one's ability to recognize and control one's emotions or reactions. Working to increase your EI might help you to make decisions that are more consistent with your long-term goals and values. Realizing that you usually react strongly when certain things happen can allow you to begin to catch yourself and temper your reaction to a level that might be more appropriate. And of course this can apply to positive emotions as well as negative emotions. Reacting in an overly positive, perhaps even in an overly euphoric manner, can lead you to make poor decisions just as easily as reacting in an overly negative, angry, or resentful way can.

> **HIGHLIGHT:** Your emotional intelligence (EI) can have just as much of an impact on your life as your IQ.

Reacting in a way that is inconsistent with your values and visions will most certainly hamper your progress toward them. Just like the saying "You are what you eat," the saying "You are what you think" is true for us all. Whether you want them to or not, your decisions will be influenced by your attitudes and reactions to the events in your life. Allowing yourself to get overly emotional in a way that contradicts your values will cause your values to flop around and cause you to flounder. Not only will these emotions change the way that you think, but they will change how other people react to you. We've talked about how a "bad" attitude can change your decisions, but what about other people's attitudes? Are you attracted to people with generally bad attitudes? Do you include them in activities or engage them in conversations? Your attitude or the perceptions people have of your attitude will influence how others perceive you and react to you.

Positivity

Spending time on your values and visions before you venture out into the next phase of your life is a great thing to do, but it is going to take a little time and effort. Hopefully you feel a sense of excitement and optimism as you try to craft a plan that will lead you toward your vision. Keeping a positive attitude will not only help you to craft that plan but will help you as you carry it out. Becoming overly down or pessimistic can cause you to lose sight of your vision and convince you that you can never attain it and ultimately give up. Remaining positive can help you avoid letting the time and effort you spent on creating your plan and implementing it go to waste.

As stated earlier, you aren't expected to be positive all of the time. If you were, I would question your mental health! Feelings such as sorrow, grief, frustration, and loneliness are natural and have their place in life. When they come, and they will, use your emotional intelligence to expect them and to deal with them. If you lose somebody or something very dear to you, it is normal to grieve that loss. Take time to do that and to process your emotions. Be true to yourself. But then you must move on. The setbacks in life will be many, but your vision should remain steadfast. Always keep that vision in your mind, and it will help to smooth out the bumps in the road that will invariably arise.

If at some point you find that you have become overly negative in your daily life, you should stop and examine the possible reasons. Your emotions and your ability to examine them can tell you a lot about where you are on your path and where that path is likely headed. Look around. Are you doing things and making choices that aren't following the values that you want to adhere to? Are you making choices that you know deep down aren't moving you toward your vision? Is something or someone having a greater impact on you than other things in your life, and if so, is it time to make some kind of a change? Perhaps you find that you aren't making as much progress toward your goal as you would like to. All of these things can dampen your positivity and need to be actively examined. You are the only one in charge of your own emotions, and therefore you are the only one who can change them. If you are feeling less than positive, find out why and carefully make some changes.

Keeping a positive attitude, while it may sound like a cliché, is a very valuable skill that will smooth out the road of life. Knowing that the bumps will come and that they are natural will help you to deal with them and keep them in perspective. Your life is a great journey and should be tackled with a sense of excitement and challenge. Don't let the negative experiences control your life and your feelings toward it. Those experiences are only a part of life, and it is up to you to determine which, if any, of your emotions you let them affect. Remember when we talked about your expectations? Do you expect that things should always go your way and that bad things shouldn't ever happen? Do you think that's realistic? And if something does happen to you or you feel like you are having a tough time, can you think of somebody out there in the world who might have it worse than you? Of course you can. And not only that, but I can just about guarantee that out of the more than 7 billion people currently on this planet, many people have been through what you are going through and came out of it okay. That thought should help you shift your mindset to one of positivity, knowing that there is a way and that your goals and vision are worthy and achievable.

Courage

Let's shift gears here and talk about an often misunderstood concept: courage. Popular culture often presents an image of being courageous as being physically tough. Action heroes in the movies have courage. Well, I think I would have more "courage" too if I could fly or was as strong as a superhero. How about courage on the football field? Do you think it takes courage to suit up and play football? Is courage doing things that are physically difficult? It can be, but that is not the whole story. Having emotional courage is just as important.

Graduation might cause many emotions to swirl through you all at once. Excitement, trepidation, hope, joy, and fear—just to name a few. How are you feeling right now? If you have been working on figuring out what your values are and picking a path to begin walking down, it would be great if you were feeling some excitement. With that excitement comes some fear, which is only natural. You are heading out into new territory and are going to face situations that you have never dealt with before. Courage is the thing that is going to help you make the choices that are true to yourself and that will keep you moving toward your vision.

So what, then, is courage? Courage is making a choice and taking an action that you feel is the right thing to do, even though you recognize that the action could cause something negative to happen. Let's break it down part by part. Making a choice without taking action is not by itself courageous. The problem with just making a choice is that nobody knows you've done it but you. Therefore, nothing negative is likely to happen. For example, if you decide that you want to sing a song at the next open mic night but don't tell anyone about it, you don't face any possible repercussions. If you tell people that you are planning to do it, you open up an array of possible reactions. Will they doubt you, laugh at you, or do some other terrible thing? If you make it through that part and then actually step out on stage alone, what then? Will they laugh or throw things? Will they hate it? Will you seize up and forget the words? What then? What will they think?

All of the thoughts that race through your mind are examples of expectations. You expect those things to happen even if they aren't terribly logical. Doubts, fears, and apprehension are often centered on the possible negative reactions of other people. You might feel that shame and rejection are extremely strong emotions that must be avoided at all costs. Sometimes these emotions, or the fear of them, aren't based in reality. Our brains are pretty good at dreaming up all kinds of terrible things and reactions that other people could have. That is probably a survival instinct still lodged in our primitive brain. Yes, they could have those reactions, but will they? How likely is it, really? Has it ever happened before? If you imagine yourself out on the stage and you make a mistake, you probably fear some kind of over-the-top negative response. But switch roles for a minute. Put yourself in the audience. If you saw somebody who was trying something new, something potentially scary, and they made a little mistake, how would you react? Would you point and laugh or throw things at them? Or would you feel impressed that the person was brave and courageous enough to step out there and try? When faced with something daunting, remember that the worst reactions from others that your mind can dream up rarely actually happen. Switch roles in your mind and try to put a rational argument in your mind for how likely it is for things to happen. It's often just as likely for things to go better than expected than for them to go worse than expected.

The last portion of defining courage is the "doing the right thing" part. Courage comes when you are faced with a choice. Having no options but to do something usually doesn't require a lot of courage to do it. Standing at the top of a 20-foot cliff above a river and deciding whether or not to jump takes some courage. If you are faced with the choice of either jumping from that 20-foot cliff into the river or being killed by the lion that is chasing you, making the jump is a pretty easy decision, though one might still be afraid. Not much courage is required. Having a choice between two values is where courage comes into play.

There is often an easy way out of a situation, a way that might appeal to one of your lower-ranking, short-term values such as "being accepted." If you do the seemingly easy thing, you don't risk rejection or ridicule. Not taking on the challenge of singing at the open mic night would certainly keep you from violating that value. Taking the challenge, however, might uphold another of your values, such as growth or advancing your career. Within yourself you know that the "right" thing to do, the thing that satisfies your more important values, is to take the risk even if it might result in rejection. The key here is that it might result in failure. It also might not. If you don't do it, you have a 100% chance of avoiding the negative outcome, but a 0% chance of gaining the benefits of success. Taking the risk and singing may or may not bring about a negative outcome. Perhaps you would have a 50% chance of a negative outcome and a 50% chance of success. Usually your thoughts and fears are much worse than the actual outcomes, and there's likely a decent chance that nothing really bad will happen at all if you do make a mistake.

Failure

Failure is a normal part of life. Without failure we would learn a lot less, and the successes that we achieved wouldn't be so rewarding. If you attempt to achieve anything of value, there will be failures. If there weren't much of a chance of failure, success wouldn't have as much value. This is the familiar scarcity idea. If everyone has something or can do something, the value of that thing is greatly diminished. If everybody had the singing talent of a pop star or the athletic ability of a professional ball player, would we pay as much to see them?

Think of failure as preparation or practice. Every time you try to achieve something and you fail, you learn a little more about it and yourself. With knowledge comes skills and confidence. Applied skills and confidence at the right time is what brings success. Success is not luck. A little luck or fate certainly helps, but it is your hard work, your preparation, and your actions that will bring you closer to your goals. Think of something that you have tried to do before but weren't successful at, at least not initially. A simple example is video games. When you get a new game you don't know that much about it or what the tricks are. With repetition, sometimes lots and lots of repetition, you begin to learn the skills and acquire the knowledge to progress through the game. What is the upside to mastering that video game? Not much, other than a sense of accomplishment. How about something a little more meaningful? In many modern societies it is the norm for men to court ladies. The men often have to make the advances and leave themselves open to rejection in order to find someone. For many men, this process doesn't start out well at all. Many young men make mistake after mistake ... woman to whom they are attracted ... reasons for this. First, the reward ... courage to ask a woman out is very high ... about love and a relationship that could ... love of your life. Failure at the task could be ... painful rejection and public humiliation. It's a to ... choice men face when desiring to approach a woman.

What happens if a young man refuses to take the risk of approaching girls? Sure, he avoids rejection, but he also doesn't learn anything from his failures. It is highly unlikely that the first girl he approaches will be his one-and-only soul mate on this planet. It might turn out that he wouldn't even like her anyway, once he got to know her better. What he could do, though, is think about asking girls out as practice. He could think about it as practice for the day when he does come across somebody who really could be his lifelong mate. He wouldn't want to be awkward or lack confidence at that point, and the only way to get to that point is to practice asking women out on dates. Ask them out, get rejected, learn from what happened, and try again. Whether it's going on job interviews, asking out women, shooting hoops, starting a business, or anything else, use failure as a tool to improve your skills and confidence so that when the moment arrives that it really matters, you are ready.

147

rely practice
, you quit first.

ATTITUDE

...ke when approaching a
...d. There are likely two
...d for having the
...h. We're talking
...rn into the
...sult in
...ugh

n situations that you
It could be a decision
complicated endeavor
that's ne..   isual reaction which is
to turn to the Interne.,   k you can also use to
navigate such situations is to think of somebody who is
good or very experienced at what you are trying to do. If
you actually know somebody, by all means ask them for
some guidance and advice. But what if you don't know
anybody who is good at what you are trying to do?
What if the Internet is not immediately available to you?
You might be surprised at how much you already know
about problem solving if you let yourself think more
freely.

We are often hampered in our decision making
because we carry our own experiences and biases with
us. It is easy and natural to try to solve problems using
our existing knowledge and skills, but we frequently
realize that we aren't nearly as successful as we want to
be in solving our problems. Life always presents
situations through which you have no good idea of how
to proceed. You've never done anything close to what

faces you at the moment. If you don't have someone around who can help you, I suggest you ask yourself for help. Ask yourself, "If I were good at this, what would I do"? That simple question will let you think beyond your own experiences and help to put the problem in a less intimidating light. Let's say you are about to go on your first job interview and you are feeling a bit overwhelmed. Maybe you even feel scared to death. Ask yourself that question, "If I were good at this, what would I do?", and see what comes to mind. Perhaps if you ask yourself what you would do if you were really good at job interviews, you could come up with a few ideas to help yourself prepare. What do you think good candidates might do for interviews? Well, they probably dress well—appropriate but well. They likely have a résumé that they have honed and had others review. A really good candidate might even do research on the person or company that they are interviewing with. I'm sure they would have practiced interviewing with somebody, a family member or a friend.

This kind of exercise can help in many situations, and it can even help if you find that you have no idea what to actually do in the situation. You might find yourself in this scenario quite frequently as you first begin your journey. If you can make no headway after asking yourself what you would do if you were good at the task in question, a slightly different approach is necessary. You'll have to broaden the question a little to move forward. Assume you got the job that you contemplated interviewing for above. Two weeks into the job you are given an assignment that is way over your head. So you ask yourself the usual question, "What would I do if I were good at this?," and you come up pretty much blank. Nada. The next step, then, would be to broaden the question and ask yourself something like "What would I do now if I were really smart?" How would a smart and resourceful person handle this situation? The answer to that might be to find a mentor, ask for help, take a course or just do some extra research online. The answers aren't going to directly help you with the task, but they will help you find a way to gain the knowledge that you need. You can ask this type of question in many ways, depending on the issue at hand. What would you do if you were really smart, honest, compassionate, funny, or romantic? What would you do if you were a good investor or a good manager? Keep this little trick in mind when you find yourself in confusing or daunting new territory after graduation. This simple exercise can help make challenging situations seem easier to handle and you just might be surprised at the answers hiding in your brain.

Confidence

Using the "what would I do if" question technique can certainly help you navigate through new challenges. Having the ability to find your way will also help to build your confidence. Confidence is an important trait that usually increases as you go through life. The older you get, the more experience you get, and that helps to build confidence. Confidence is an interesting trait in that it is tied to how you feel about yourself and your abilities, but we often relate it to how others perceive us. You might be confident in your physical abilities but lack confidence in social situations. Understanding a bit more about confidence and how it affects you can help you to make decisions that better align with your vision.

Confidence can be described as the belief that you are correct, taking the best approach, or expecting the best outcome. If you are confident going into an interview, it means that you might be feeling or thinking several things. You might feel or think that you are doing the right thing even if you don't expect to get the job. You might feel or think that you are just the right person and are expecting to nail the interview and be offered the position. You might feel confident in yourself and your abilities in general and feel that the outcome of the interview is not the most important thing in the world. In the worst case, it's a practice run. Confidence in each of these situations might be warranted if there is a good chance of the outcome happening or coming true.

Overconfidence or arrogance is believing that you are worthy and correct, and expecting a certain outcome when you really don't have a shot or a good reason for feeling that way. You can be confident in an outcome or in yourself, but still acknowledge that failure is possible. Overconfidence is not acknowledging that there is even the chance of failure. There is almost always at least some chance of failure. Confidence is recognizing that chance and still pressing forward. Overconfidence ignores that chance and therefore doesn't plan for it, learn from it, or react appropriately to it.

Perhaps one of the most damaging things to our confidence is the weight that we place on other people's opinions and the reactions we expect from them. Here we see that confidence and courage are related concepts. While courage requires an action, confidence is an internal feeling or belief. Just as courage is required when we anticipate a negative reaction from others, confidence is keeping the opinions of others in perspective. You don't want to entirely discount the opinion or reactions of others, but you certainly don't want others' opinions to run your life or control your emotions. Having no regard for the thoughts or reactions of others can be described as being a sociopath, and you probably don't want to be one of those. What you need to do is find a balance between believing in yourself and considering the thoughts and reactions of those whom you trust.

Confidence can be gained or increased through a couple of means. First, it naturally increases with the amount of experience that you have with a given task or activity. Practicing or actually putting yourself into real situations will cause you to gain the skills and knowledge to succeed at them in the future. In addition, failing at those tasks will prepare you to handle failing at them again if that should happen.

152

Knowing what to expect when something doesn't go the way that you hoped can give you extra confidence to make the attempt next time. Knowledge of what might happen eliminates the unknown, which is usually far more frightening than the actual outcome. Second, you can increase your confidence by thinking through the possible outcomes, either positive or negative. We often have a generally negative feeling when we are faced with something that we aren't experienced with or are unsure we can do. You might find that if you truly think through what would happen if you failed at the task, the actual outcome is not as bad as your first gut reaction made it out to be. Thinking through the events, outcomes, or reactions that might result will also give you time to figure out a response to them. Being prepared for failure can be just as much of a confidence builder as being prepared for success.

Of course, one of the ways to prepare yourself and build confidence is to acquire a group of supporters. These people can be family or friends, but they should be trusted, honest people. Having these people to practice on, get advice from, and lean on will give you the feeling of a safety net. What better way to go through this next phase of life than to have a safety net? When you do seek the opinions of these trusted people, make sure that they tell you what they honestly feel or think in a constructive way. Ask them for their real opinions. It can end up as a rude shock if your supporters tell you that you are ready for something when they really feel that you are not. Life usually doesn't care about your feelings and won't sugarcoat its response. Get their real feelings early to avoid a potentially nasty surprise later.

As you work toward building your own safety net, look for opportunities to provide that same support to someone you care for. Helping somebody else work toward a goal and providing encouragement and a positive outlook will help you to feel the same way. Emotions and states of mind are very contagious. Bad moods breed bad moods, and positive outlooks breed positive outlooks. If you want to feel more positive, help somebody else to feel that way.

Action

Okay, now you have built up some confidence, worked on your courage, have a positive outlook, and figured out that failure is just a part of the road you must travel toward success. What happens now? Take action! Get out there, make plans, find your vision, and go after it. None of your goals or your dreams will ever come true if you don't do something to achieve them. Nobody is going to hand you anything. All great journeys start at the beginning with step one. Put on your shoes, walk through the doorway, and head on down the road.

Few things in life will turn out exactly as you planned them. That's just the way it is. But that is no reason to not try to do something. You'll often find that even if you don't end up exactly where you wanted to be, you might be somewhere just as good or even

154

better. If you don't work toward your goals at all, you won't end up anywhere different than where you are right now. Making a plan and acting on it is the best way to achieve your vision.

You have probably heard of the "80/20 rule," known as the Pareto Principle. It is a common concept in business management used to describe how a lot of things in life seem to work. It is used to describe the idea that 20 percent of things account for 80 percent of the cost or effort or weight or whatever. It is also the notion that 100% usually never happens. Sometimes you just have to get to 80% and call it good. Trying to figure out something to 100% certainty will lead you to analysis paralysis, and you will spin your wheels forever and never take step one. For this next phase of life after graduation, think through your values, goals, and vision. Make a plan with some short-term goals or milestones, but don't try to get it to 100%. If you try to figure out every detail or make provisions for every possible outcome or failure, you won't ever get off the couch. Create a good plan, not a perfect plan, and get started. Your path and your plan will change and develop as you go, but you must get up and go at some point.

THINK WHERE YOU'RE GOING

8

Them

God grant me the serenity
To accept the things I cannot change,
Courage to change the things I can,
And wisdom to know the difference.
-The Serenity Prayer

Them

Having control over your own thoughts, emotions, actions, and dreams is all well and good, but you can't get through life without interacting with other people. There is a funny saying that goes like this: "I've figured out the group of people who I really don't like. It's others." While I hope that this doesn't represent your thoughts, you will inevitably be forced to interact with people in situations in which friction will arise. Some of these people will be those whom you choose to be around, such as friends. Many of them will be people whom you are "forced" to be around, such as family, coworkers, bosses, and neighbors. Understanding a little about the motivations and reactions of yourself and other people will help you to deal with conflicts between people. You will also learn why many conflicts happen and how to avoid them in the first place.

The Forced

Let's start with the easier group to deal with. This group of people is made up of the ones that you are "forced" to interact with. These are (1) the people in your workplace—your boss, your employees (if you have any), and your coworkers, and (2) the people in your family. Most of this group will be found in the workplace after your graduation. If you continue with school of some sort, you will also have students and faculty to deal with. You won't exactly get to choose who these people are since they just come with the package, so to speak. If you are having a difficult time with these folks and keep interacting with them, you are choosing another value over the comfort or convenience of not dealing with them.

WORKPLACE

The traditional workplace is full of people who you must interact with on a daily basis. If you haven't had a job up to this point, you can think of it as group work, like you probably had in school. It just goes on for a very long time. Few, if any, of these people will be people whom you would ordinarily choose to hang around. Even so, the vast majority of people are just normal people. They are, like you, trying to get by in life and realize a few of their own dreams. The workplace will have three basic groups of people: bosses, employees, and coworkers. Smooth interactions with all of these groups takes some empathy and lots of communication. Most conflicts arise due to a lack of information or communication from one or both parties.

> **HIGHLIGHT:** Most conflicts between people are caused by a lack of information and/or poor communication.

Boss

The boss group is the group of all management that is above you, including your direct supervisor, all the way up to the head of the company. If you work for a small firm, your supervisor might be the head of the company. If you work for a huge corporation, this group can be much larger, perhaps in the tens of people or even more. Bosses can be a tricky group to deal with. You will not only have to consider their motives and viewpoints, but you will also have to use your courage and confidence to a greater extent with them than when dealing with the other groups. The key to a good relationship with your boss is to make things easier for him or her, to complete your tasks, and to make him or her look good when that's possible and appropriate.

Making things easy for your boss doesn't mean that you need to do his or her job. What it means is that you need to understand that a boss has a lot of responsibilities, and you don't want to be a problem employee. Your boss has you and other direct reports to consider, his or her own duties to accomplish, and his or her own bosses to please. Being a good team member is all about helping others work efficiently while you complete your own tasks. Think of the kind of person you would want to have working for you and try to be that person. What traits would that person have? Perhaps those traits might be hard-working, honest, skilled, and having good communication and people skills. You can always ask yourself the "what would I do if" question again. What if you were a great employee?

Bosses don't like surprises, so keep them in the loop on your progress and issues, especially if something is not going according to plan. And a lot of things won't go according to plan. If your boss knows ahead of time, he or she can deal with the issue earlier and make adjustments as required. Letting your boss know what's happening also allows your boss to take some responsibility for the issue if it does become a larger problem later. If you surprise everybody at the end, you are the only one responsible for it. If you were a star relay runner on your college team, what would happen if you knew you had a pulled muscle but didn't tell anyone until the last second? Your coach and your team would have had no time to adjust and make corrections to the game plan, and the team's problems would rest entirely on your shoulders. That is not how teams should work.

A fine line needs to be walked when you have issues and dilemmas at your job, and this is where people can stumble. You don't want to run to your boss with every little detail. They have hired you to deal with most of these. You also don't want to continually raise a red flag if the problems either aren't that severe or have a low risk of happening. Don't cry wolf all the time. That just gets distracting. What you do need to be careful of is letting yourself think that you can always solve problems before the boss finds out. It is a natural tendency of many people to conceal issues longer than they probably should. Concealing issues lets you postpone any possible negative reactions from your boss or coworkers, such as a reprimand if you made an error, extra overtime to catch up, or just appearing less competent than you would like. Some issues you might be able to fix on your own without anybody finding out. Some you won't. The trick is being able to know when you need to come clean. Having regular, honest dialogues with your boss will help to keep him or her up-to-date. Usually a boss will recognize and appreciate an honest, hard-working employee who is trying to make a difference. Most bosses expect that some level of mistakes and issues will happen. Just keep communication flowing, consider your boss's perspective, and things will go much smoother.

Employees

This section on employees will apply to you in two ways. First, you will naturally start your career as an employee. The information presented here will be good to know so that you understand how you as an employee fit into the overall framework of the company that you work for. Eventually you might find yourself promoted at work into a managerial role, or you will go out and start your own business and hire some help. At that point you will have employees or direct reports. We will just call them employees here. Some of these people you might inherit with the job, and some of them you might be able to hand-pick and hire yourself. Having multiple employees means having to deal with multiple people. Each of these people will have different skill sets, personalities, and motivations. Some of them will be terrific right out of the gate, some will need a little time and guidance to mature, and some will be acceptable, at best. Even those whom you hire yourself might not turn out to be what you expected during the interview process.

Good employees, whether it is you or someone working for you, are engaged. They have a reason to be there other than just the paycheck. True, all employees work for a paycheck, and that is usually the number-one reason that they keep coming back. Good employees, however, have other reasons to come to work every day. They have values and visions that fit with the work that they are doing, and they find doing their work beneficial to them, aside from the monetary compensation. Finding out what your employees' values and motivations are will help you to tailor their work for the best possible outcome. Building a team that is engaged in their work and working because of something other than the paycheck is a very powerful skill. Creating a team of employees that functions well is creating a system. That system is more valuable than any one team member, and it should create value for the company. Many people go to work and perform tasks with little control over others. Those people are almost like a commodity in that they can be replaced with relative ease. Finding people to manage them well is more difficult and has greater consequences, and therefore those positions pay better. The people who can create and manage teams are in high demand and will be more difficult for you to find.

Good employees are fun to work with. They are engaged, positive, and normally perform their tasks well. When you have these people you should recognize them. Money is always in fashion, but that is not the only thing that drives good employees. Find out what else they thrive on and try to reward them with it. It might be further research into a particular field, possibly more education, public recognition or branching out into a new part of the company. Find ways to help and service your good employees and they will perform well for you.

Not-so-good employees are much more challenging to deal with. They are so great a challenge that many supervisors and managers ignore the issues until something drastic happens. Doing this is not only a disservice to the employee, but it is bad for the company, team, and you as a manager as well. By waiting to address issues, you are wasting time. You are wasting the time of the employee who could be working more effectively and wasting the time of the team that is slowed down and distracted. Often you might find that when you address the issue directly with the employee you discover a disconnect or lack of communication. They might not know exactly what is expected of them or where and how they fit into the bigger picture. They might not know the effects that their work is having on other people. You might also find out that there is another issue that you are unaware of that is a cause of the lower-than-expected performance.

Perhaps you might find that this type of work or environment is not what really engages this person, and you might conclude that some kind of change is needed. That change could be anything from a slight shift in job responsibilities to helping the person find a new job. In the end you might have to fire him or her if the person does not choose to find a job that better suits his or her goals and interests. Certainly it can be a difficult thing to do, but as a compassionate person you should do what is likely in the best interest of that person and the rest of the team. As a boss you have a job to do, goals and objectives to meet, and the job of developing and guiding your team. Don't take firing somebody lightly, as it can have a large impact on that person and on your team. You have probably invested a lot of time into that person and losing his or her knowledge might be a short-term detriment. But at times it must be done for the success of the team and sometimes for the success of that person in the future.

Here is one last note about employees and your relationship to them. While it is normally good to be an approachable boss, you need to have some boundaries. These boundaries are sometimes called professional boundaries. Problems can arise when your employees or direct reports consider you more of a friend than a boss. They might appeal to the friend side of you and cause you to make decisions that you would not normally make as a boss. Even if you truly think that your decision making is not affected, it can still appear so to other people. Resentment and strife can build between these friends who are direct reports and the rest of your team.

It should go without saying that romantic or sexual relationships with your employees should be strictly avoided. If your relationship goes south, these types of relationships can lead to big problems legally, such as sexual harassment suits or worse. And don't think that you can hide these relationships for long as there are no secrets at work. Even if you did manage to keep it quiet, it can blow up big time if you have a nasty breakup. Your best bet is to avoid these at all costs. If that person is truly your soul mate, a simple job change for one of you won't matter in the long run.

Coworkers

The last group of people who you will frequently deal with at work consists of your coworkers. Coworkers are the people with whom you interact who are close to the same level as you in the company, but who are not your direct reports. In other words, you don't oversee them and they don't oversee you. Your coworkers can be a great source of new friends, since you will be spending a lot of time around them. Sometimes these bonds can grow very strong, especially if you are in a high-stress job environment or achieve a significant milestone as a team. Similar to soldiers in battle, or sports teams in contests, you can form friendships that have been tried, tested, and endured.

When you first enter the workplace, if that is the path that you choose for yourself, you might find that you spend a great deal of time away from work with your coworkers. You probably will still be single or at least have no children at first, so your social life will be in high gear. Early in your career you are building up your network. Your coworkers, the people who you hang out with today, might be the next VPs or CEOs tomorrow. Keep in touch with the talented ones as you move through your career. You never know where you will all end up.

FAMILY

When it comes to your family, the only one that you get to choose is your spouse. Well, at least in most modern countries. The rest of the family is related to you whether you like it or not. Your family and perhaps a few very close friends will be the ones whom you interact with for your entire life. Everyone else will come and go, but family is family and they are here to stay.

It is natural to find some members of your family more appealing than others. Even though you are all related, you are still unique individuals and everyone has their own opinions and personalities. Some of your family might not have been your favorites growing up, and you might prefer to keep your distance. That is all well and good, but keep an open mind toward family as you move past graduation. Life has a funny way of changing your perspective, and you might come to realize that what you thought was true when you were younger might look different after some time in the "real world." The pressures of work and providing for family might have made your parents seem aloof a few years ago. Once you get out and experience what they were going through yourself, you might just change your opinion. Keep an open mind. Your family can be a great safety net for you, and you can be that for them, so try not to alienate anyone unless you have a really good reason to do so.

The Chosen

The chosen group includes all of the people with whom you interact by choice. While you might in many ways choose to interact with your coworkers because you choose to work at your place of employment, the chosen group contains the people you really want to be around for no other reason than you like them. These are your friends, affiliations, your spouse, and your acquaintances. This group of people is an extremely powerful force in your life for good and sometimes for bad. You see, the people who you choose to be around say a great deal about you and about where your life might be headed. Here at graduation you have a great opportunity to review your current pool of chosen people and decide if changes need to be made.

Friends

"Friends" is such a powerful word. The friends you choose will determine much of your life's path, almost more than your own mind will. Humans are a social species, and we need interaction with our tribe to reach our full potential. A sense of belonging, acceptance, encouragement, protection, and shared passions are the things that a group of friends provides. A close group of friends can almost act like a single entity, with thoughts and actions that wouldn't occur to each individual alone. We build on our emotions and experiences as a group and sometimes seemingly get swept away in the frenzy of it all. That frenzy, that oblivion to the outer world, our own unique thoughts, and the possible consequences of our actions can lead to great triumphs or tragic disasters.

A group of friends can have a powerful impact on your decisions. Friends provide a means to satisfy the very basic, primal values of acceptance and protection. Doing something that might jeopardize that, even if that action supports another of your important values, can be a terrifying thing to do. If your friends don't share your values and, to some extent, your vision, you probably won't achieve your vision. You will be much more likely to achieve the values of the group, no matter what they are. The world is full of tragic stories of young people getting into serious trouble even though they knew that what they were doing was wrong. It went against some of their values and they knew it. They did terrible things because of the people they were with, people they called friends. The power of the group, the power of belonging and acceptance, can make people do things that they normally would never dream of doing.

The world is not made up of all bad people and gangs of thugs. The incredible power of a group can lead you to do amazingly good things just as easily as it can lead you to do terrible ones. The difference is which group of friends you choose to have. Look back at the past few years leading up to graduation. What type of friends did you have? Surely you all shared some common interests, but did you really share common values and visions? Did you ever find yourself secretly disagreeing with what the group was saying or doing? If you stick with that group do you think you are likely to achieve the life you really want? It can be difficult and scary to make a change in your friendships, but it might be necessary if their values don't line up with yours. Now could be a great moment in your life to make those changes.

Just as positivity can be a contagious attitude, optimism and your thoughts in general can pervade your circle of friends. Over time you could be the one that helps your friends change their thoughts and actions and bring them closer to your own. You can either be the guiding light in your group, stick with the group if it's working for you right now, or strike out and find a new group. If you are moving away after graduation for more school or a job, or even just for a fresh start somewhere new, be careful who you choose to be friends with. Don't be afraid to test-drive friends and move on to new ones if you find that your new ones are drawing you in the wrong direction. Think about who you are and who you want to be, and try to find friends who are better than you at those things. Just like playing sports with people who are better than you can improve your game, hanging around people who are smarter, kinder, more compassionate, or more productive can help you as well.

Acquaintances

All friends start out as acquaintances. Acquaintances are people you have met and know a little, but whom you don't know well enough to call friends. They might have the potential to become friends if they are social acquaintances, or they might just remain acquaintances if you know them in a business or professional capacity. In social situations, acquaintances are usually harmless, but do pay attention to their circle of friends if your interactions continue to evolve.

One type of acquaintance that might be new to you as you enter the workforce or business world is the mentor. A mentor is someone who is either on the same road you are but further down it than you are, or someone who is already quite successful in the area that you are pursuing. A business mentor can help you to chart the path of your career or your new business venture. A life mentor or life coach can help you to stay focused on your values and your path and show you ways to maintain a balance between them. As you put your plans together, consider the option of reaching out to someone who can be a mentor to you. In return, once you are ready, consider mentoring others who are coming up behind you. Not only will you feel good by helping somebody else, but being a mentor will reinforce in you what you already know. Teaching is a great way to retain and focus on the things that you know.

Affiliations

Your affiliations are groups that you belong to or relate to, but the people in them aren't necessarily your friends. The people you know in these groups are similar to acquaintances in that you might know the individuals but aren't friends with them, at least not yet. If you are religious, your church might be a good example of an affiliation. You consider yourself part of that group and share its values, but the other church members might not necessarily be your friends or even acquaintances. Other examples of group affiliations can be the fan base of your favorite sports team or music group. Of course, your political stance could be strong enough to cause you to choose to be affiliated to one political party or another, such as the Democratic or Republican parties.

Affiliations can be good in that they provide some sense of belonging to a larger group or cause than you experience in your day-to-day life. You might have values, perhaps long-term values, that are shared more with affiliations than with any other groups, such as family or friends. Once again, however, care should be taken to ensure that those shared values are really the ones that you want to be important values. If you find that you are making decisions that you normally wouldn't or aren't heading in the direction that you desire, take a look at your affiliations and see what kind of effect they are having on you. The news media frequently reports on cults or other secretive groups, particularly when members of such a group, after years of membership, decide that the values of the group are no longer ones that they want to be associated with. Such individuals often decide to leave the group and to end their affiliation with the group. Their action occasionally causes the group or its leadership to attempt to force them to remain in the group or to harass them. This sort of thing happens in extreme cases. The point, however, is that there is tremendous power in affiliations, and our great desire to belong and be accepted by others can blind us sometimes to the true nature of a group. Examine your current affiliations and compare their goals and values to those you hold. Do this when you form new affiliations as well.

Spouse

Your spouse will probably be the one person in your life who has the greatest influence on you from here on out. Your husband or wife will start out as an acquaintance, turn into a friend, and then become something more when those romantic feelings start to happen. That acquaintance will become your lifelong friend and partner. Some marriages last well over 60 years. That is a long time to spend with one person, and the effects can be profound. Living in such an intimate way with somebody for that length of time will have its moments of joy and its moments of frustration.

In the United States, nearly half of all marriages fail. Why do you think this happens? They often fail due to a change in values or vision, or a realization that the values and visions weren't the same from the start. They might also fail due to a lack of communication. As we mature into adulthood we change rather rapidly. Just as you are very different from the way you were five years ago, you will probably be different five years from now. Your values might change in their order of priority, or you might change your value set altogether. Getting married early can increase the risk of either you, your spouse, or both of you making dramatic changes in your values. As you know, your values affect who you are, how you act, what you do, and who you want to be around. This is not to say that getting married when you are young dooms your marriage to failure, but the fact that people often do dramatically change is something to keep in mind. Are you both mature enough and similar enough to have a good chance of staying together in the long run?

This phenomenon of changing values and visions, sometimes called "growing apart," can happen much later in life as well. While changes in values and vision

174

happen fairly quickly when you are young, older people tend to change more gradually. This gradual change can be tolerated for a while, but eventually some people find that the differences are too great. Sometimes this realization can be triggered by a singular event such as a child leaving home, a change in a job, or financial troubles.

There are many reasons a marriage works well, but a core reason is the spouses having similar values and visions. You two are a team that is tackling life together and should have a similar mindset on many key issues. When you start to get serious with someone, make sure that you have compared your values and visions. If the other person hasn't put much thought into his or her values and vision, but you have already done so, you might have to help the other person think about those issues. Listen to what the other person says and watch what he or she does in life. You should be able to pick up patterns that suggest how the other person's values are ordered. Talk seriously about your vision for the future with him or her. If the other person reaches his or her goals, are you going to be happy being with that person? Is the opposite true? Marriage can be a beautiful and powerful thing in your life, so it is best to make sure you have a solid foundation that makes both of you happy and helps both of you reach your goals.

Once you find your spouse and tie the knot, he or she will become many things to you—including friend, lover, supporter, and mentor. In a good marriage you will both be all of these things and more to each other at different times. Someone that important to you deserves respect and honesty. In a good marriage, you will respect your spouse's opinions, desires, needs, and vision. You will support your spouse because you want him or her to succeed. You will be honest, almost to a fault. Just as in the workplace, strife in a marriage can come from one party in the relationship missing or not understanding information from the other party. In a good marriage, you will be open and honest, and you will trust that the person you married will be respectful to you as well. If you're married and you can't give respect and honesty, or you don't trust your spouse to do the same, you are in for a rough ride.

Part 3

Your Journey

THINK WHERE YOU'RE GOING

9

Get Started

...Life, Liberty and the pursuit of Happiness.
-U.S. Declaration of Independence

Get Started

We've covered a lot of ground in the preceding eight chapters. Let's figure out now what you want to do and what you need to do to get started. By this point I hope you have evaluated your values, crafted a vision or two, perhaps identified some friends and affiliations that no longer fit with who you are deep down, and are ready to go. If you haven't done those things, I suggest you do them now and then come back to this point in the book. If you don't do them now, you leave your life in the hands of your fickle unconscious mind, or worse, in the hands of other people. Neither always has your best interests at heart.

Idlers

Are you looking for a life that is carefree, with few responsibilities and lots of personal time? Do you find that money and wealth don't mean much to you? Do you care little about what compound interest is? If so, there is a great path for you. The idler path is a great choice for those who are quite content with the status quo and have no ambition beyond their current state of affairs. Endless video games, a wealth of available entry level jobs, and plenty of like-minded friends await you if you choose the idler group. The catch here is that if you don't actively choose one of the other paths, you probably will get the idler path by default. The idler path requires the least amount of planning, preparation, and thought of all the groups.

The values shared by most idlers are skewed toward short-term gratification and entertainment. What idlers lack is any kind of long-term vision. For whatever reason, and there are several, idlers prefer to not look very far into the future and have no concrete vision of where they want to go or who they want to be. They might have vague visions or dreams of being rich or successful, but they don't put any plans or short-term steps together in order to attain their vision. One thing going for the idlers is that with a typical lack of money and low available credit, they normally can't get themselves into too much debt or overburden themselves with material things.

So what does it take to become an idler? Pretty much nothing. Unfortunately, you might have already ruined your chances of being a "successful" idler by reading this book up to this point. Your mind is currently poisoned, but if you give it enough time you will forget about this book and others like it, and you might settle back into your idler ways. Forgo any further study of life, finances, or biographies of people you find successful and you should have smooth sailing.

There are a few things that you really should know about, however, to prevent a really big mistake. Being an idler is all about the status quo and maintaining a comfortable equilibrium. Making a big mistake could upset that comfort level, so you need to watch out for a few things. As a member of a modern society there are a few must dos. You have to live somewhere, make at least a small amount of money, and you have to eat. Essentially, you have to fulfill your most basic needs. There are some nice things to have like personal transportation and some health care, but it really depends on what is important to you and how hard you want to work for them.

Let's tackle the first one, which is a place to live. Your options are limited considering your income level, so you are either choosing between living with your parents, crashing with friends, renting, or being homeless. Let's assume being homeless isn't your choice. That leaves your parents, other relatives, friends, and renting. Living with your parents can be virtually free, since the incremental cost to them is fairly low. You might have to accept a few rules that aren't in your favor, but there is a price to pay one way or another. Ideally you could find a way to get a separate entrance into the home, which would create an apartment-type atmosphere without the usual rent payment. This could be a win–win situation if your parents continue to claim you as a dependent for a while and get a tax break. Add in a little bit of additional schooling and you could make that last a few more years.

Renting your own place or with roommates can be a lot of fun, but it does come with more responsibilities. First, you have rent to pay. Rent, as you know, is a set amount that you pay usually every month. That rate and other details are covered in your rental contract that you sign prior to moving in. Make sure you read your rental contract and understand the details. You might have to pay a stiff penalty or make up for your delinquent roommates if they fail to pay their share of rent. In order to get an apartment there is typically money due up front, which includes a security deposit and the first and last month's rent. For an idler this can be a significant chunk of change, so you might want to start saving some money, including any graduation money that you might receive.

If you are having trouble with the full rent payment and buying groceries, there are community or government programs that can help you cover some of the costs. Section 8 housing, food stamps, and other social services can be used to help pay for your easy-does-it lifestyle. If this is your preferred way of life, you might want to do a little research to find the best place to live. Each state, county, and city has different rules and programs, so look around to find the best fit for you. Don't expect lavish living, but don't expect to work any overtime either.

Workers

As a graduate, you are already a couple of steps down the road to becoming a member of the workers group. To be a worker requires having a job as step one, and that usually requires a high school diploma/GED or any number of higher-education diplomas. These can be one-year or two-year certifications, associate degrees, bachelor degrees, masters degrees, or even PhDs. Even if you are just graduating from high school and considering your job choices and the option of further education, try to focus on something that you find of interest or enjoy. If you are planning to do some type of work for the next 40 years, you should find at least some level of enjoyment in it.

Be careful about the common idea of "do what you love." While you might find that you are able to make a living doing what you love, it is unlikely that you will achieve great wealth that way. What are the chances that what you love to do is something that a lot of other people need but few other people want to do? Value comes from scarcity, so be careful about just doing what you love. For example, if you love flowers, you could open up a floral shop. You might find some level of success, but your flower shop likely won't make you very wealthy because the demand is somewhat low for the service you offer, and many people would like to start that type of business. Be sure that your plans match up with your values and vision of success, and do some research to verify things before you jump in. Flowers might not create a lot of wealth, but you might still be personally successful.

HIGHLIGHT: Having passion for what you do can help you to succeed, but doing what you love is not a guarantee of financial success.

184

You might find that you have a vision of success for yourself in the future but don't know quite how to get there. Figuring out what you want to do with your life can be a very perplexing activity. There are times when you must separate what you do from who you are or who you want to be. Many successful business owners have reached their goals of wealth and security through less-than-glamorous types of work. If you struggle to identify the exact type of worker you want to be, that's okay. Treat the work that you end up doing as a step down your path to success and not as the destination. Remember, jobs can come and go, you can change careers midstream as long as you are still working toward your long-term vision of success.

To get a plan started, follow the tips from earlier chapters and examine your values. After that, craft a vision of where you want your life to go and what it should be like. This vision will serve as a guide, but it can certainly change over time. In order to be a member of the worker group, you need to take action towards achieving that vision and meeting your goals.

The next step after graduation is to pick a type of work or specific area of focus that will be something that you enjoy in some way and will likely lead toward fulfillment of your vision. Make sure, though, that your choice of work and the effort you plan to put in actually match your vision. For example, a vision of a large mansion on the beach and lots of expensive things probably won't match reality if your job choice is that of a teacher. If your values and vision are more along the lines of a comfortable living in a small, close-knit community surrounded by friends and family, being a teacher might work well for you. It's okay to dream big, but be realistic about your choice of work and the lifestyle and vision you are likely to achieve with it. The worker group seldom ends up financially wealthy, and if they do, it happens after many years of working, saving, and investing. The road is long, but it carries relatively low risk with a moderate reward at the end called retirement.

Once you have selected a profession or career, you have to either get a job, if you are ready, or get more education to prepare yourself. More education is the easy step here. If you need more education, find another college or program, apply, get accepted, figure out a way to pay for it, and do the work. Paying for it can take many forms, such as cash up front, working during school, taking out loans through several sources, or use of grants or scholarships. If you decide to take out loans, read through the sections in this book about credit and loans and be sure you understand what you are signing up for. If you can't afford to start or can't get into a program right away, don't fret. Get a job of some kind and start to save a little. Keep an eye on your vision and continue to try to get into the program that you feel you need.

Getting a job calls for an action plan that starts with finding a job opening. Whether you are searching locally or nationally determines the best ways to find a job opening. Local jobs can be easier to find because you will know the area and the employers. Many local jobs are only advertised locally, and you can find out about openings through word of mouth or just chance sightings of help wanted signs. Searching nationally can take several different approaches. Of course there are the big job boards, such as national newspapers, Internet sites, or social media. There are lots of jobs posted out there, but there are also lots and lots of people competing for those jobs. If they are easy to find for you, they are easy to find for everyone, and everyone will be applying for them.

Another option is to use a recruiter. A recruiter will essentially try to sell you to a company that is looking for people with your skill set. Companies usually pay recruiters directly when they hire candidates, so the service is free to you. Recruiters can be found online or in your local telephone or business directory if you live in a bigger city. One caveat, though, is that recruiters typically look for people with specific skills or experience levels, so it might be harder to use them if you are just starting out.

Last, but not least, is to hit the metaphorical pavement. To do this, identify the type of work that you want to do and then find companies that engage in that type of work. Search for those companies and inquire either through their websites or through phone calls if they have openings or anticipated openings that you might be a fit for. Not all positions are posted on job search sites, and a little extra effort on your part can pay off.

There are many resources to help you write a résumé and prepare for an interview once you find a job that you want to apply for. On the day of the interview, dress a little better than you think you normally would for the job on a daily basis. If it is a professional office-type position, a nice suit is appropriate. If you are applying for something more casual, such as a warehouse worker, a nice shirt and pants might be more appropriate. The key is not to dress more casually than you should, which could give the impression that you don't care. Overdressing, on the other hand, can make people think that you don't understand the job or are trying too hard. As always, be on time, open, honest, and friendly. Most of all, be yourself. If you put on an act or say things you don't believe in, you might end up in a job that really doesn't fit you, and you won't be happy. Use the tips from earlier chapters about confidence to keep your nerves in check.

Once you land a job, you will have to fill out a bunch of forms and might be faced with decisions about benefits, taxes, and other matters. Common items that you might encounter include the following:

- **I-9 Employment Eligibility Verification:** Show forms of ID to verify your identity and authorization to work in the U.S.
- **Non-disclosure Agreement:** You agree not to reveal confidential company information to outside entities.

- **Non-compete Agreement:** You agree not to work for a direct competitor for a period of time after you leave that company.
- **Insurance:** Health, Dental, Life, Disability, etc.
- **Health Savings or Flexible Spending Accounts:** Programs to use pretax savings for qualified expenses.
- **W-4 Tax Withholding:** Determines how much of your pay is deducted for taxes.
- **Direct Deposit:** You might elect to have your pay deposited directly into your bank account instead of receiving a paper check.
- **Retirement Plans:** Defined Benefit or Defined Contribution Plans, like 401(k) and 403(b) plans.

Landing your first job gets you started on your journey. Keep your goals and vision in mind and refer to them often. You don't want to get too distracted during life's ups and downs, so remind yourself of where you want to be in five years. Most of all, enjoy the ride. Your life is what is happening right now, today. Don't live in the past or too far in the future or you will miss the memories that you should be making right now. A good work ethic, minimal stumbles, and a good attitude will see you through your 40-year working career. The end has a good chance of being close to what you envisioned, with a little retirement nest egg set aside.

Controllers

Choosing to become a controller is not to be taken lightly. It takes more focus and determination than joining the ranks of idlers or workers. If you pick this group, be prepared for a lot of work and uncertainty, but your reward could be substantial. Controllers are people who have a good handle on their values and vision and have a system set up to achieve those goals.

Your first step, therefore, is to examine your values and set your vision. Since the definition of success lies solely with the individual trying to achieve it, you are free to pick any goals and vision that you care to. Success does not mean lots of money, if that is not what you value. However, controllers are often trying to gain freedom and long-term security, which can often be achieved through increased wealth. Creating and controlling a system that provides wealth might allow you to focus on your other values, such as family, charity, adventure, and so on. Wealth can also provide increased security in the form of improved health care, insulation from the ups and downs of the job market and recessions, and ownership of basic requirements, such as housing.

Recall in the chapter on values that people in the controller group understand their values and have set them in a relative ranking. This ranking does not change easily or quickly. Even if you work very hard now to examine yourself and come up with a value set, it still might change slowly over time as you grow and mature, and as the path of your life unfolds. That is fine and expected, but you must have a starting point now. It is easier to make small corrections or iterate an existing plan as you go than it is to try and create the perfect plan at the start. But to do that you must have an "it" to iterate from.

Your second step is to create a system that employs leverage to achieve your goals. Leverage is a way to achieve more with less effort on your part. Workers stick close to a one-for-one trade ratio (time traded for money), while controllers try to maximize the ratio. You can do that through physical systems or machines, through employees, or through other means.

There are many resources available to help you determine what forms of leverage to employ. Methods for using systems and leverage include the following:

- Starting a business
- Investing (stocks, art, etc.)
- Becoming an author
- Investing in real estate

There are many more ways to use leverage, and if you're interested in being in the controller group, you should continue to explore other resources on this topic. Remember, the goal for each of the four activities in the list above is to create a system or machine that creates value or wealth for you. Starting a flower shop that you have to work at 10 hours a day is not a controller-type system. That is more like a job. If you don't show up, you don't make money.

Early sacrifices, if you want to call them that, are needed to build the foundation that you need to succeed as a controller. Instead of spending all of your money and time on other values like enjoyment and entertainment, you might have to study more and work harder. These are only sacrifices for you if they are closely competing with your long-term values. If that is the case, be careful that you don't slip into the worker group, as that is one of their hallmarks. As you study and learn more about successful people, you might find that doing what they do is enjoyable to them in many ways. They are driven to work at their systems because the end result, their vision, is so powerful and meaningful to them. Giving up some of the typical worker activities is not difficult for them because they believe in their vision and they are spending time on their top-ranked values.

Educating yourself, finding like-minded friends and mentors, and consistent practice are all needed to build a successful system. Practice is required because failure is expected. Don't be afraid of it. Failure is never permanent until you quit. If you keep learning and working toward your goals, failures are merely steps that you learn from. You are essentially teaching yourself.

The following checklist can help you get started in building a successful system:

- ✓ Examine your values and write them down on paper in order.

- ✓ Define your vision.

- ✓ Break your vision down into achievable goals, step by step.

- ✓ Periodically review these and your progress toward them.

- ✓ Find like minded friends and perhaps a mentor.

- ✓ Study your chosen field or path in a variety of ways.

- ✓ Make a plan while remembering that 80% is often good enough.

- ✓ Get started.

- ✓ Expect some failures, learn from them, and treat them as steps to success.

- ✓ Change your plan when needed, but not very often.

Creating systems that provide wealth will require not only knowledge of how that system or industry works, but knowledge of money as well. Financial literacy is something that you will need to begin to acquire immediately. Being able to code a website is a skill that you might need to create the system, but it won't help you maintain and grow your wealth. You will jeopardize your system if you don't understand how it operates, how to grow it, and how to protect it. Even if you entrust others with some of the details, don't give up complete control and don't take your eye off of it. Accountants and managers could be vital to operating your system, but they might not have your best interests at heart all of the time. In addition, choices and decisions might need to be made that you have a differing opinion of. If you are a true controller, you probably think a little differently than they do as workers. Stay true to your values, your plan, and your vision.

Expect to be different. Expect to be abnormal. If normal is defined as what the majority of people are doing, you don't want to be normal. Normal in our societies is the worker and idler groups. Controllers are abnormal. Embrace your new-found abnormality, seek out others to share the journey with and don't do normal things. There is a reason that there is the so-called "1 percent" group. They often do what the other 99% don't do.

10

Changes

There is nothing noble in being superior to your fellow
man; true nobility is being superior to your former self.
-Anonymous

Changing Categories

Understanding your values, setting goals, and crafting a vision are all important actions to help you through your life's journey. Often, however, our vision is something that is set some distance into the future, perhaps years or even decades away. During that time we can stray from our path, or our vision can change entirely. Just like driving a car requires lane changes and moving into exits, your drive through life will require adjustments.

A change in the path that you are on can be initiated by a number of things. Your values and vision could just change slowly over time through experience and maturity. On the other hand, large life changes like falling in love, having a child, getting injured, or experiencing something very emotional can make your current vision obsolete and shift around your values. These big life changes or events are clear and obvious points in our lives where making changes makes sense. Having a child might suddenly change your vision of success from a big mansion outside L.A. to a small house in a quiet community full of kids. Many of the people who join the military and travel outside of the United States are affected by what they see and experience. These things can have a dramatic effect on how they see the world as a whole and what their values are.

Gradual changes in your life are a little tougher to recognize and to deal with, which is why you need to stop and look around every once in a while. No matter if you think things are going great or if things clearly are not, you should take time to look at your life, your values, and where things are headed. Have you been making progress toward your goals, or are you stuck spinning your wheels? Are you sliding backwards? It takes a concerted effort to look at your life when you aren't prompted to by some large, sudden event. It is easy to not think about these types of things and get comfortable in your daily routine, even if this routine is not what you wanted your life to be like. Life tends to gain a certain momentum, and it takes effort and action on your part to make changes if you want or need to.

HIGHLIGHT: Sometimes changes in your life can occur over time and are hard to notice. Take time occasionally to examine your life for these subtle shifts that might have gone unnoticed.

Throughout this book we have focused on three main groups of people in society: idlers, workers, and controllers. These are not the only groups out there, but they are the most relevant ones to talk about when you are just graduating high school or college and trying to figure out your life. Another group that was mentioned earlier in the book is the strugglers group.

Whereas idlers make conscious choices to live the way that they do, strugglers are typically in survival mode, where making rational, conscious choices is impaired or impossible. Severe health or mental issues, depression, and addiction are some of the things that can cause people to land in the struggler group. In some cases, you can find your way out of the struggler group and into one of the others, as in the case of people receiving treatment for depression or addiction. A severe health issue might be cured partially or completely so that it no longer controls your entire life. If you find yourself in a survival situation in which you feel you cannot make rational decisions about your life, you might need to seek outside help. Most of the other groups can make changes in their lives through their own personal introspection and planning. They don't necessarily need the help or guidance from other people, although receiving such assistance can be very beneficial. Struggler group members often cannot find their way out of that group without the help and guidance of others. Sometimes they need the help of professionals. If you think you are in this group or find yourself there someday, seek help. There is no shame in asking for help when you need it, and we all need help from time to time. There is help out there in ways that you might not see now or expect. Reach out and get started.

Look around at your life now and do so again on a regular, periodic basis. When you look around, ask yourself if you are happy. Are you content? Are things headed in a direction that you like? Are your actions matching the values that you want to have as your most important values? If not, it is time to change something. Reexamine your vision and see if it still holds true. If so, look at your values. Write them down again and try to order them the way that you think they should be. Now look back at your actions over the past week, month, or year. Do your actions and decisions support those values, or have you been placing something else closer to the top of the list?

Changes will have to come from you. You are the only one who knows what is important to you and what your vision really is. Nobody forces you to go to a particular job, hang out with certain people, or spend your personal time doing specific things. All of these choices are yours, and you are driving your life. It might be hard, but being honest with yourself is the best way to start to make changes. That little voice in the back of your head has a finely tuned B.S. meter, and it knows what your truth really is. Even if you can rationalize your decisions with some crazy reasoning that half-convinces you, that little voice still knows the truth. Listen to that little voice. Follow its guidance.

Changes can happen in small ways and in big, life-altering ways. Whether you find yourself as an idler, worker, or even a controller, changes can still happen. Remember that these groups are not clear-cut, and there is a gradient from one to the other. If you don't like your current situation or the direction in which things seem to be headed, determine the scope of the changes that you think you need to make. Some changes could be big, like getting divorced and moving to a new city. Some could be small, like starting a new habit of saving $20 a month or only playing video games on Saturday instead of every day. Making a change in your life as a response to your dissatisfaction can have an interesting effect. The first change can be tough, but the second can get easier, and the third might be easier yet. That first change, whether simple or profound, can start a trend with increasing momentum. All it needs is for you to have the courage to take that first step.

There are many ways to make changes, so let's talk about a few as examples. Your life, as we've discussed, can be affected by your knowledge or education, action, values, plans, friends, environment, money habits, and perceptions. As a graduate, you have just completed making a huge change in your knowledge and education. Is this the education that you need to fulfill your dreams and goals? If not, where can you get the information that you now need? Do you need more courses, or do you need to get some real-world experience? Gaining more skills or knowledge is fairly easy as long as you find the time to do it. If it is high on your value list, you will find the time to get it. The technology available today allows you to access people and information in incredible ways that you can fit into your life. Make use of your time and the tools around you to get what you need to be successful.

Knowledge and skills are worthless, however, if you don't use them. You need to take action to make some changes. If you look around and find that some changes might be in order, I'll wager that you already know what those changes probably are. Think them through and then make them happen. Taking action not only makes a change in your path, but also makes a change in how you think and feel about yourself and your life. Taking action lets you take back some control of your life, and that can be a huge boost to your psyche. Doing something for the betterment of yourself is a big attitude and confidence booster, and who doesn't like that? Remember, if you do what you always do, you'll get what you always get. If you want things to be different in your life, you need to do different things.

Changes in four areas, in particular, can have a big impact on which group you are in. These areas are financial literacy, friends, planning, and attitude.

As covered earlier, money isn't the most important thing in life, but it does allow you to achieve more goals and visions than if you don't have it. Getting it, growing it, controlling, and protecting it require some financial literacy. Would you attempt to drive a race car or expect to win a race if you didn't know how to drive? The same idea applies to money. Changing your knowledge level of money and how it works will increase your chances of not crashing and burning. Read books, take a class, ask around, practice with small amounts, or do whatever it takes to learn more about it. As always, though, beware of scams. If it seems too good to be true, it probably is too good to be true.

The people who you associate with, whether friends or your spouse, will have a huge impact on what you do and how you think. Don't underestimate this effect. If they aren't headed somewhere that you want to go, or their values don't match yours, you need to figure out a way to remove their influence on you. There are over 7 billion people in the world. Surely you can find a few like minded souls. Even if you think you won't be able to do so, get started down your own path by yourself, if necessary. Eventually you will stumble across others like you, and you are more likely to find them if you are doing the things that are important to them as well as to you.

By now you should be convinced that planning is important. It is important not because it outlines where you are going and what you need to do to get there, but because it gets you started and gives you something to shoot for. Without a plan, without some kind of schedule and desire, you probably won't even get off the couch. Even if you do get off the couch, what are the chances that you will just happen to end up somewhere that makes you happy and feels successful? They are quite small indeed. Remember that your plans don't have to be perfect, so write one down and get started. Plans are powerful if you take action on them, and few people do. Create your vision, break it down into a plan of smaller steps, and get started.

Lastly, your attitude about yourself and about life will be your constant companion. Having confidence and a positive attitude makes making changes in your life easier. It also allows you to reach your goals and be successful sooner. Do you know people who are happy and positive? Do you think that they think of themselves as successful? Which came first, the positive attitude or the happiness? If happiness is one of your values and goals, you can start on the road to that goal today. Nobody else can make you feel anything. Your emotions and your feelings all come from inside of you. Decide how you want to feel and what is important to you, and then focus on those things.

Making Changes

Any good plan will still need to be reviewed from time to time. As you begin on your journey, remember to take the time periodically to examine where you are and compare it to your plan for achieving your personal version of success. If you feel that things in your life are a little below your expectations or subpar, perform the following 6 steps to help you make the changes that you need to get back on track. SUBPAR is a handy acronym to help you remember these steps in the future.

See:

Look around. Are you happy? Feel successful? Headed in the right direction?

Understand:

Why not? What are you doing? Who are your friends? How do you think and feel?

Balance:

Weigh these things against your values and vision. If you keep doing them, are you likely to get where you want to be?

Plan:

Make a plan to correct the things that don't match.

Act:

Act on that plan. Break it into smaller pieces. Ask for help when needed.

Repeat:

Look around again from time to time.

11

Final Thoughts

Success is measured not so much by the position that
one has reached in life as by the obstacles which one
has overcome trying to succeed.
-Booker T. Washington

Final Thoughts

Graduation is a big accomplishment and opens the door to the rest of your life. Walking through that door likely fills you with excitement, fear, optimism and uncertainty. As a high school graduate you might not have a clear plan to follow after this step. If you are graduating with a higher degree, you probably have at least a rudimentary plan, which is why you pursued the degree that you did. Either way, it is crucial at this stage to take some time and decide where you would like your life to go. If you don't make a plan for it everybody else will or, worse, nobody will.

Having read this book puts you into a special group of people. The world is full of people who are wandering through life with no real plan and no real understanding of how things work. You have at least taken the first step to control your own destiny. You now understand that nature and societies operate through systems, and that systems only run when there is a disparity in some way or another. You are free to choose where you want to fit into these systems. Having this basic understanding should give you some sense of confidence as you venture out into the world. Knowing how things work and how you fit into it will help you to make changes to your life if you find that you aren't headed toward the vision that you desire.

Planning, goals, and a vision are also key to making your life into what you want it to be and achieving success in whatever way you define it. Go after your goals and vision using your values as your guide, but don't forget to live in the present. Life requires a balance to satisfy all of your important values. Spending all of your time and energy pursuing long-term financial security, for example, while neglecting your family values will cause problems for you and those you love. Examine your values, give them structure or order, and work to satisfy all of the important ones, not just the top one.

When you set out to determine your values and your goals, be very careful how you interpret what society calls normal. If you look closely, you will find in many cases that the images portrayed don't always match reality. Set your goals and your vision based on what is important to you and not what you think is important to other people. Trying to fulfill somebody else's values will be difficult at best and is better left up to that person instead. If other people are not happy with you, they need to examine their own value set. As we said, you are in control of your own feelings and emotions, just as other people are responsible for theirs. A common trap of the worker group is trying to fit a perceived image of what success should look like. It is a trap because success is only defined by you, not by anybody else or by society. Figure out what values are important to you, craft your vision, and take action. If success to you is driving fancy cars that you can't afford, then go after it. If success to you is driving fancy cars that you *can* afford, make your plan and make it happen. No matter what, when you take action and reach goals, or make no plan and take no action, the situation that you end up in is yours to own. Nobody makes you do anything, so you shouldn't blame anyone else if you end up somewhere you don't want to be.

Life should be about the journey toward your goals and vision. Of course, we all know that nobody gets out of this alive, so you should at least enjoy the trip. The journey that you take and the memories that you make with those you care for are just as important as where you ultimately end up. For many, and maybe for you as well, success is just being happy in the moment. Whatever your value set ends up being, it will probably contain some values that can be satisfied on a daily basis. Don't forget about those as you strive for the future. Besides, plans change, visions develop, and your memories along the way might end up being more precious to you than the ultimate goal that you thought was so important here at graduation. Work on creating your garden, but don't forget to smell the roses along the way.

There is no right or wrong way to go through life. None of the groups—idlers, workers, and controllers—is better or worse than the others. The group that's "right" for you depends on what you want out of life and what you define as successful. The world system needs all kinds of people for it to operate, and there is plenty of room at every level. But remember that your actions and thoughts will determine your true place even if you pretend to be in a different group. Pick your place and start working toward it.

FINAL THOUGHTS

Once you figure out your values, set your vision, and start working your plan, it's time to think about giving back to somebody else. You probably have friends or relatives, or know people younger than you who are struggling. Guide them along gently as they learn about how things really work and decide where they want to fit in. If they think about it, they just might get to where they really want to go.

THINK WHERE YOU'RE GOING

Notes

1. "U.S. Census Bureau, Statistical Abstract of the United States: 2012," Table 270, accessed January 15, 2015; http://www.census.gov/compendia/statab/2012/tables/12s0270.pdf.

2. "U.S. Census Bureau, Statistical Abstract of the United States: 2012," Table 299, accessed January 15, 2015; http://www.census.gov/compendia/statab/2012/tables/12s0299.pdf.

3. "U.S. Census Bureau, Statistical Abstract of the United States: 2012," Table 587, accessed March 29, 2015; http://www.census.gov/prod/2011pubs/12statab/labor.pdf

4. "U.S. Census Bureau, 2012 Annual Social and Economic Supplement to the Current Population Survey," accessed January 15, 2015; https://www.census.gov/hhes/www/poverty/publications/pubs-cps.html.

5. "Household Debt in the U.S.: 2000 to 2011," U.S. Census, accessed January 15, 2015; http://www.census.gov/people/wealth/files/Debt%20Highlights%202011.pdf.

6. "Distribution of Household Wealth in the U.S.: 2000 to 2011," U.S. Census, accessed January 15, 2015; http://www.census.gov/people/wealth/files/Wealth%20distribution%202000%20to%202011.pdf.

7. "National Marriage and Divorce Rate Trends," National Center for Health Statistics, accessed January 15, 2015; http://www.cdc.gov/nchs/nvss/marriage_divorce_tables. htm.

8. "U.S. Light Vehicle Sales," Wards Auto, accessed January 15, 2015; http://wardsauto.com/datasheet/us-light-vehicle-sales-december-2014.

Your Notes

My vision is:

My top values are:

My goals for this month are:

My goals for this year are:

My goals for five years from now are:

My positive and supportive friends are:

My negative and distracting friends are:

Made in the USA
Lexington, KY
13 January 2016